When We Gather
A Book of Prayers
for Worship

When We Gather

A Book of Prayers for Worship

Year B

A Collection of Worship Aids
Based on the Lectionary
Prepared for Trial Use
by the North American Committee
on Calendar and Lectionary

James G. Kirk

With art by
Corita Kent

THE GENEVA PRESS
Philadelphia

Book design by Alice Derr

First edition

Published by The Geneva Press®
Philadelphia, Pennsylvania

PRINTED IN THE UNITED STATES OF AMERICA
9 8 7 6 5 4 3 2 1

Library of Congress Cataloging in Publication Data

(Revised for volume 2)

Kirk, James G.
  When we gather.

  Includes index.
  Contents: [1] Year A — [2] Year B.
  1. Prayers 2. Liturgies. I. Title.
BV250.K57 1983   264'.13   83-14221
ISBN 0-664-24553-6 (pbk. : v. 2)

Contents

Foreword

The responsible planning of worship, viewed as a disciplined time in the presence of God, is an equitable cost of discipleship. That cost is gladly paid when the benefits are so obviously rich. And now that God's people around the world are gratefully recovering the ancient habit of ordering worship within an agreed-on pattern of Scripture lessons, worship is increasingly a recognizable whole whose parts fit comfortably together. It is astonishing that in a short span of fifteen years the major Christian churches in the West have come closer together in relating Scripture and worship than at any time within the preceding millennium. Moved by that momentum, the Consultation on Common Texts (CCT) in March 1978 convened representatives of thirteen churches in the United States and Canada to make proposals for achieving as much consensus as possible within the familiar three-year lectionary pattern.

To achieve that end, the CCT set up the North American Committee on Calendar and Lectionary (NACCL), which over a period of five years agreed on a basic calendar, a schedule of psalmody, and a revised table of lections that took into account the acknowledged critique of the Vatican II lectionary and its subsequent adaptations by the major Protestant denominations. The NACCL report* has now been approved by the CCT and recommended for trial use in the several churches. It is on the basis of this *Common Lectionary* that Dr. Kirk has prepared his excellent treasury of worship aids for each of the years in the three-year cycle. Year A is already in print and in use throughout the churches. Response to this resource has been enthusiastic.

*Common Lectionary: The Lectionary Proposed by the Consultation on Common Texts (New York: The Church Hymnal Corporation, 1983).

Year B is presented here in the lively expectation that it too will be eagerly greeted and gratefully put to use.

In many ways it was easier for the NACCL to achieve agreement on the proposed revisions of the lections themselves than on the ordering of the calendar. Concurrence on the lections does not achieve the desired level of synchronization if the agreed-on lections are read on different Sundays. The solution finally arrived at was to employ the "propers" enumeration already in use by the Roman, Methodist, and Episcopal churches, which omits unneeded sets of lections at the beginning rather than at the end of the post-Pentecost period. (When Easter is late, fewer sets of lections are needed.) This calendar decision was made after *When We Gather* (Years A and B) was tabulated for printing. Use of the following table, which shows the "proper" number and inclusive dates for Sundays after Pentecost, will ensure synchronization with all churches that follow the *Common Lectionary*.

YEAR B

Proper No.	Inclusive Dates	Gospel Reading
3	May 24 to May 28 (if after Trinity Sunday)	Mark 2:18–22
4	May 29 to June 4	Mark 2:23 to 3:6
5	June 5 to June 11	Mark 3:20–35
6	June 12 to June 18	Mark 4:26–34
7	June 19 to June 25	Mark 4:35–41
8	June 26 to July 2	Mark 5:21–43
9	July 3 to July 9	Mark 6:1–6
10	July 10 to July 16	Mark 6:7–13
11	July 17 to July 23	Mark 6:30–34
12	July 24 to July 30	John 6:1–15
13	July 31 to August 6	John 6:24–35
14	August 7 to August 13	John 6:35, 41–51
15	August 14 to August 20	John 6:51–58
16	August 21 to August 27	John 6:55–69
17	August 28 to September 3	Mark 7:1–8, 14–15, 21–23
18	September 4 to September 10	Mark 7:31–37
19	September 11 to September 17	Mark 8:27–38
20	September 18 to September 24	Mark 9:30–37
21	September 25 to October 1	Mark 9:38–50
22	October 2 to October 8	Mark 10:2–16
23	October 9 to October 15	Mark 10:17–30

24	October 16 to October 22	Mark 10:35–45
25	October 23 to October 29	Mark 10:46–52
26	October 30 to November 5	Mark 12:28b–34
27	November 6 to November 12	Mark 12:38–44
28	November 13 to November 19	Mark 13:24–32
29	November 20 to November 26	John 18:33–37

The resources provided in *When We Gather* are useful not only for planning corporate worship for a congregation but also for small-group or private devotions. Reverent use of these resources can enliven any gathering with a rich awareness of the "great cloud of witnesses" that always surrounds Christians at worship.

LEWIS A. BRINER, *Chairperson*
The North American Committee
on Calendar and Lectionary

Advent, 1983

Preface

Perry LeFevre writes, "Prayer is what human beings can do to develop an attitude of openness and sensitivity together with a focusing on goals for change so that God can work in and through their lives for transformation" (*Understandings of Prayer*, p. 59; Westminster Press, 1981). *When We Gather* provides assistance for the people of God in developing that attitude of "openness and sensitivity."

For example, prayer should begin by *rehearsing* what God has done. This rehearsal establishes the context of God's faithfulness throughout the ages. Rehearsal involves discipline, which in this case means setting aside for a moment our cares and needs in order first to give God praise and thanksgiving for what God has done and continues to do. To begin prayer by rehearsing puts whatever follows in perspective.

The psalmist confesses that the theme of praise shall be "the glorious splendor of thy majesty, . . . thy wondrous works" (Ps. 145:5). He writes, "All thy works shall give thanks to thee, . . . and all thy saints shall bless thee!" (145:10). Thus the people of God are exhorted to praise God with all their hearts, "in the company of . . . the congregation" (Ps. 111:1). The chronicler reminds us that greatness, power, glory, splendor, and majesty belong to God, "for all that is in the heavens and in the earth is thine"; to God then is to be given thanks and praise of God's glorious name (I Chron. 29:11, 13).

Rehearsal occurs as well through thanksgiving. Indeed, thanksgiving to God is portrayed as the richest gift of sacrifice the believer can bring (Ps. 50:14, 23). Thanksgiving for what God has done rehearses just how God will empower us to do whatever is necessary. Psalm 66:16–20 portrays well how God hears prayer and does not withdraw the love and care that we need. Just as

11

with praise, so also with thanksgiving: rehearsing what God has done sets the context for what prayer may lead us to do.

The next moments should then be spent in *reflection*. That is to say, how is God speaking to us in the present? Prayer needs a framework, and that framework should be God's continuing revelation and encounter. Reflection helps us take the time necessary for God to intrude.

As God intrudes, changes occur. There is potential for priorities to be reordered and renewed significance to be given to time, for the mundane to be transformed with elements of the sacred, for God's Holy Spirit to empower our lives. H. Richard Niebuhr wrote that God's revelation occasions a permanent revolution in our lives, through which "we understand what we remember, remember what we have forgotten, and appropriate as our own past much that seemed alien to us" (*The Meaning of Revelation*, p. 81; Macmillan Co., 1941).

Prayer should have the framework of reflection on a continuing basis, for even in our prayers we are so busy talking, daydreaming, or thinking about what we ought to be doing that God in Jesus Christ scarcely has a chance to say anything to us. That is why I chose the lectionary texts as the framework for God's revelation and encounter. They allowed me the necessary time to reflect on what God's priorities might be; they renewed the present in the light of a past full of God's faithfulness, goodness, saving power, unfailing love, and truth; they countered mundane concerns, fears, temptations, and sinfulness with Christ's act of redeeming love on behalf of all creation; and they had a way of permeating whatever occurred throughout the day with the empowering presence of God's Holy Spirit.

So after moments spent rehearsing God's glory in praise and thanksgiving, and time taken to reflect on what it is that God would have us do, prayer evokes a *response* through transformation and commitment. One cannot earnestly pray to God and expect to continue to do as one pleases. The openness and sensitivity that occur through praise and thanksgiving, together with a focusing on goals for change caused by God's revelation and encounter, will allow God to work in and through our lives for transformation.

Prayer is not abstract, nor can it deal for long in generalities without becoming specific. Prayers speak of real needs, felt joys, confusing ambiguities, and perplexing issues. God's word is always addressed to a particular time and a particular situation. That is why the prophet Isaiah could be so specific:

The Lord GOD has given me the tongue of a teacher and skill to console the weary with a word in the morning; he sharpened my hearing that I might listen like one who is taught. The Lord GOD opened my ears and I did not disobey or turn back in defiance. . . . I did not hide my face from spitting and insult; but the Lord GOD stands by to help me; therefore no insult can wound me. (Isa. 50:4–7, *NEB;* cf. 49:8)

Throughout *When We Gather,* the prayers seek to make us mindful of the gifts bestowed by God's graciousness. The people are reminded of the particular need to be addressed. Transformation is sought so that those gifts may be used in unique ways to alleviate particular situations. The end of prayer is the commitment of the faithful to go forth and serve, filled with the fullness of Christ.

How can I repay the LORD for all his gifts to me? I will take in my hands the cup of salvation and invoke the LORD by name. (Ps. 116:12, *NEB*)

Unless otherwise indicated, Scripture quotations are from the Revised Standard Version. The word "Lord" has been changed to "God," and masculine pronouns for God have been eliminated, except in quotations from *The New English Bible (NEB),* which have not been adapted to remove exclusive language because of copyright consideration. In Scripture quoted from the Revised Standard Version, the inclusive word has simply been substituted; in quotations from *The Book of Common Prayer (BCP),* the substituted words are in brackets. For the convenience of the leader of worship, material from the Revised Standard Version that has been used in the calls to worship and the litanies is not enclosed in quotation marks. Scripture references in prayers and litanies are given only when the passage cited does not occur in the day's reading.

J.G.K.

Epiphany, 1984

who shall
level
uneven ground

and
make a plain
of the
rough places

FIRST SUNDAY OF ADVENT

Lectionary Readings for the Day
Ps. 80:1–7; Isa. 63:16 to 64:8
I Cor. 1:3–9; Mark 13:32–37

Seasonal Color:
Violet

Advent is a time of expectant watching, watching for the One who like a potter molds us and shapes us in accordance with God's will. The people are told to be ready, for they know not when the hour will come. They are to be about their tasks, performing functions appropriate to the gifts they have received. It is a time of anticipation and preparation, of being alert to God's presence among us. Watch!

Call to Worship
LEADER: Give ear, O Shepherd of Israel. Stir up thy might, and come to save us!
RESPONSE: Restore us, O God; let thy face shine, that we may be saved!
LEADER: Open thou my lips.
RESPONSE: And my mouth shall show forth thy praise.

Prayer of Praise and Adoration
O Shepherd of Israel, you open our lips; our mouths give you praise. You shepherd your flock, gathering us from our wanderings, assembling us in Christ's name to learn of your will. Your covenant names us, your law guides us. The prophets attest to your promise that we shall not be forsaken. With great expectation we watch for your unfolding plan of salvation. Be present with us and guide us toward the truth in Christ's name.

Prayer of Confession
UNISON: Almighty God, "we have all become like one who is unclean, and all our righteous deeds are like a polluted garment. We all fade like a leaf, and our iniquities, like the wind, take us away." We fail to call on your name; we don't stir to take hold of your plan for us. Yet you are our God. "We are the clay, and thou art the potter." May all that we do be the work of your hand.

Assurance of Pardon
LEADER: Hear the words of Paul when he writes: "God is faithful, by whom you were called into the fellowship of God's Son,

Jesus Christ." By God's grace you will be sustained to the end, and through Christ's mercy you will be found guiltless in the day of our Lord Jesus Christ. To God be all praise and glory.

Prayer of Dedication

God of unchanging truth, your promise is eternal, your benevolent care spans the ages. We come with our gifts to be molded in accordance with your purposes; we offer ourselves to be shaped by your will. Fill us with wisdom, and make us vessels of your truth. Make all that we do an outpouring of your goodness, spreading compassion on the afflicted and care to all who may be in need.

Prayer of Thanksgiving and Supplication

O God our Redeemer, by your grace you enrich us in speech and knowledge. We can pray with all confidence that through Christ you hear us. You fill our days with the presence of your Holy Spirit; we receive guidance for the decisions we must make. Waking or sleeping, we are enfolded with your protection.

You bid us watch for signs of your reign. Open our eyes to behold your presence in all parts of our lives. Keep us from putting you on the fringe of existence, from turning to you only when we are in need. Keep us forever aware that you accompany us in all our journeys; help us to make you preeminent in all that we do. Let others see in us the firstfruits of goodness and mercy, and themselves be brought to know you through deeds of goodwill.

You tell us through Christ to be ready, since we know not when the hour will come. Keep us from putting off until another time the discipline that will make us better disciples. Make us willing to break the comfortable routine and dare to start ventures that will test our obedience. Surround us with those who have made a similar commitment, so that they may teach us. Help us to seek their assistance and to learn of their ways.

You send us out to be about our tasks. Go before us to guide us, and stay behind us to prod us. Live within us as God who fashions our being, as Christ who keeps us from falling, and as Holy Spirit in whose name we can do all things.

Lectionary Readings for the Day

Ps. 85:8–13; Isa. 40:1–11

II Peter 3:8–15a; Mark 1:1–8

Seasonal Color:
Violet

A message is sent to prepare the way. The tone is set for what will be involved. John comes, crying in the wilderness, "Make straight the way of the coming Messiah." There shall be baptism with water; Jesus will baptize with the Holy Spirit. There shall be confession of sins; Christ will himself be the means of repentance. Heralds proclaim what is to come, offering a foretaste of what to expect.

Call to Worship

LEADER: Let me hear what God will speak, for God will speak peace to God's people.

RESPONSE: Surely God's salvation is at hand for those who fear God, that glory may dwell in our land.

LEADER: Yea, God will give what is good, and our land will yield its increase.

RESPONSE: In God's righteousness let us worship, that we may walk in God's way.

Prayer of Praise and Adoration

O God of peace, your way is sure and leads to salvation. You send your Son, the promise of life eternal; your Holy Spirit guides us to truth. We hear your heralds proclaim the path of obedience, and receive your abounding grace, making firm our footsteps; we know that all is made ready to follow you faithfully. We praise you in thought, word, and deed. By your mercy, affirm your unending love for us, and in our worship make us alive in your promise.

Prayer of Confession

UNISON: O God of forgiveness, with our tongues we speak evil against our sisters and brothers. By our actions, we disobey your commandments. Hostility is bred through our suspicion and envy; anger continues in spite of Christ's peace. You open our eyes to his righteousness, yet we remain blind to the truth of his reconciling presence. Forgive our deliberate misuse of your mercy, and in Christ hear our prayer.

Assurance of Pardon

LEADER: Isaiah speaks of God's comfort, of pardon of iniquity, and of the One coming who shall level uneven ground and make a plain of the rough places. All the earth shall know that God's judgment is tempered by Christ's presence and peace on our behalf. In him we have assurance of pardon.

Prayer of Dedication

O God of our righteousness, in whose sight a thousand years are as one day, we come this day offering our gifts. Use them to spread the news that Christ comes so that all may dwell in peace. Help us to break down whatever hostility divides our sisters and brothers, and hear us as we dedicate ourselves anew to becoming your agents of reconciliation.

Prayer of Thanksgiving and Intercession

Herald of good tidings and Proclaimer of peace to the nations, we thank you for all those who bring a foretaste of your righteousness. Your word is a beacon that illumines your goodness, bringing hope to a world that is weary of strife. The message has gone out throughout all of history that you will judge the nations with fairness; you will lead your people to a more glorious day. We yearn for the time when our days are more tranquil. Be with all those who still dwell amid tension. Ease suspicion that breeds hostility, leading brothers to speak out against brothers, and sisters to mourn the death of those who are victims. Make us impatient with mere words that speak of peace. Help us to substitute words with actions, and to take those first steps to heal divisions and reconcile differences.

We give thanks for leaders who boldly proclaim the end to warfare and strife. Give them courage to match their convictions, and firm resolution to remain steadfast in their commitment. Give us determination to acquaint ourselves fully with the issues, and keep us from making hasty judgments in complex situations.

We pray for those whose very lives depend upon decisions made elsewhere. Give them some sense of justice and dignity. Let us who are the church of your Word, Jesus Christ, join with them in their plight and their promise, uniting to bring about a new day. Enlarge our world to include them in the decisions we make. Make us more sensitive to the truth that how we live determines whether others survive. Bring closer the time when the way of love shall be recognized as your way, and the nations shall confess that you alone are God.

Lectionary Readings for the Day

Luke 1:46b–55; Isa. 61:1–4, 8–11   *Seasonal Color:*
I Thess. 5:16–24; John 1:6–8, 19–28   *Violet*

The call to repentance is the start of discipleship. Passing through the waters, the believer emerges with newness of life. The waters of baptism symbolize that rite of passage whereby old ways are forsaken in favor of a commitment to God's justice and righteousness. John baptizes in the wilderness, bearing witness to the Light that illumines God's will, even Jesus Christ, the Way of justice and peace.

Call to Worship

LEADER: My soul magnifies the Sovereign One.
RESPONSE: And my spirit rejoices in God my Savior.
LEADER: For God who is mighty has done great things for me.
RESPONSE: And holy is God's name.

Prayer of Praise and Adoration

Your deeds are mighty, O God, and your name is to be blessed forevermore. Holy is the One who comes in your name. As we gather in Christ's name, so fill us with the Holy Spirit that our words may tell of your marvelous deeds. Let our songs of praise rise to you as our response of love and adoration.

Prayer of Confession

UNISON: O God of the covenant, have mercy upon us as we make our confession. The afflicted await good tidings. The brokenhearted would have their wounds bound. The captives still yearn for freedom, and those who mourn remain to be comforted. Forgive us who fail to follow Christ's call to faithful ministry; restore us and make us worthy to serve in his name.

Assurance of Pardon

LEADER: Sisters and brothers, hear what Paul writes concerning the assurance we have in Christ: "May the God of peace . . . sanctify you wholly; and may your spirit and soul and body be kept sound and blameless at the coming of our Lord Jesus Christ. The One who calls you is faithful, and will do it."

Prayer of Dedication

God of peace, in Christ you bring light to illumine the nations. He makes your will known to all who believe. We come in response to his call to us, seeking to follow and fulfill his commands. Accept the gifts we offer as symbols of our commitment; sanctify them wholly, that they may be used as you desire. Mold us and use us as instruments of your will. May all that we do be in accord with the gospel of him whom you have sent.

Prayer of Thanksgiving and Supplication

Eternal God of grace, you comfort those who mourn, heal the afflicted, deliver the captives, and bring hope to those who despair. You are a God who bends to the needs of your people, surrounds them with tenderness, and lifts them out of despair. We give you thanks for sending us Jesus, who walked this earthly way and himself was tormented and afflicted with pain. Through him we can face those trials that await us, and reach out to others with words of good cheer. We give you thanks for your Holy Spirit, who continually guides us, inspiring us to greater service on behalf of all your people. We are frail and prone to weakness, yet you remain our source of inspiration and strength.

Clothe us in the garment of Christ's promised salvation and send us out to proclaim renewed hope to your people. Make us bold to witness to the truth of your righteousness, and fearless in the face of our adversaries. Protect us from accusations against us, and help us to counter charges intended to weaken our resolve. Keep firm our commitment to act on behalf of your justice, so that the weak can themselves receive courage to stand.

Garb us with the splendor of your Spirit, and renew our spiritual core. Make us faithful in our study of Scripture, disciplined in prayer, and wholly abandoned in our response to the gifts that you give us. Deliver us from the frenzied pace of the world about us, so that we may find time to reflect on your will for our lives. Arm us with your mercy and strengthen us by your grace, so that we can be truly free to obey Christ, whom we serve.

FOURTH SUNDAY OF ADVENT

Lectionary Readings for the Day
Ps. 89:1–4, 19–24; II Sam. 7:8–16   *Seasonal Color:*
Rom. 16:25–27; Luke 1:26–38   *Violet*

Mary finds favor in God's sight. Filled with God's Spirit, she will conceive and bear a Son. He will be called holy, and his reign will be everlasting. He will call people to obedience, to a life of witness on behalf of God's will. In him the fullness of God's revelation will reach culmination, as he teaches his followers the extent of God's love. Mary carries within her the embodiment of God's promise and is blessed with the living presence of God's grace.

Call to Worship
LEADER: I will sing of thy steadfast love, O God, for ever.
RESPONSE: With my mouth I will proclaim thy faithfulness to
              all generations.
LEADER: (Let us worship God.)

Come and be worship God, who brings comfort and hope.

Prayer of Praise and Adoration
Your steadfast love endures forever, O God; your name is heralded throughout the land. Songs of rejoicing are heard in your sanctuary as hymns of praise proceed from our mouths. You fill your people with the gift of your Holy Spirit; you send forth a Savior with the promise of new life. You are our God, and great are your wonderful deeds. We worship you now in great adoration.

Prayer of Confession
UNISON: O God of compassion, have mercy upon us. You send forth your Spirit, yet we ignore your counsel. Christ dwells among us, yet we fail to obey him. We sing of peace on earth, yet hostility continues. Angels herald good tidings, yet we commit evil deeds. Forgive our deliberate and indirect misuse of your graciousness, and make us worthy to receive Christ in our lives.

Assurance of Pardon
LEADER: God, who is just and gracious, has sent Jesus Christ into the world to redeem us from sin. As we turn to God with contrite hearts, Christ intercedes on our behalf. So with assurance I can say to you, in Jesus Christ we are forgiven.

Prayer of Dedication

Source of life and Bringer of light to the nations, you provide for all our needs. We bring your gifts in response to your goodness. We thank you for sending Christ into our midst. Use what we offer, to enlighten all people to the truth of his salvation, and bless all our endeavors as we seek faithfully in Christ's name to do your will.

Prayer of Thanksgiving and Supplication

Eternal God of the covenant, whose faithfulness endures from age to age, we pray knowing that you will not forsake us. You have come to us as a child born of Mary, full of promise and grace. Through the power of the Holy Spirit, this Holy One, Emmanuel, reveals forevermore the depth of your wisdom and the wonder of your salvation. As we commit our lives to him and learn of his will, we give you thanks for your manifold gifts, which embrace all of life.

We pray that by your compassion you will sustain the lonely, give hope to the despairing, and fill the fainthearted with courage. Help us to comfort, encourage, and strengthen others as we minister in Christ's name. Make our very presence a source of solace, and the assistance we offer a means of succor.

May your patience become an example to those who struggle for righteousness and await the results, and may your sending of the Prince of Peace be an incentive to us and all people who yearn for peace. Fill us with the vision of the prophet Isaiah, who proclaimed release to the captives, liberty to the oppressed, and good news to the poor.

Let your wisdom sustain all who worship you, providing counsel and guidance as your children mature in the faith. Broaden our vision to behold how we may serve you more obediently amid the complexity of our world. Keep us attuned through our own study to your enduring revelation.

Your salvation comes in an infant born of a woman. We give thanks for Jesus Christ, that he calls us to be members of his household of commitment. Empower us to respond obediently to those tasks set before us, and make us worthy to be called his disciples in all that we do.

and wonder

CHRISTMAS EVE/DAY

Lectionary Readings for the Day

Ps. 96; Isa. 9:2–7

Titus 2:11–14; Luke 2:1–20

Seasonal Color:
White

As shepherds watch over their flocks, an angel appears, bringing glad tidings of great joy: A child is born who will bring peace to the nations. A multitude gather to witness the event; they are filled with wonder and awe at God's merciful deed. From this time forth and forevermore, justice and righteousness shall flow like streams of living water.

Call to Worship

LEADER: Sing a new song; tell of salvation each day!

RESPONSE: We will declare God's glory among the nations, God's marvelous works among all people!

LEADER: Bring tributes of praise and ascribe glory to God!

RESPONSE: That God's sanctuary may be filled with majesty.

(Author's adaptation)

Prayer of Praise and Adoration

O God of peace, to you we ascribe all honor and majesty, beauty and strength. You bring forth a child whom we call blessed, upon whose shoulders rests the destiny of nations. You give us the gift of life everlasting, a wonderful counselor who shall guide all your people. With shepherds and angels, we lift our voices rejoicing: All glory to you in the highest, and on earth peace among those with whom you dwell.

Litany of Affirmation

LEADER: Be not afraid; for behold, I bring you good news of a great joy which will come to all the people.

RESPONSE: God's grace has appeared for the salvation of all.

LEADER: For to us is born a savior, who is Christ the Lord.

RESPONSE: God's grace has appeared for the salvation of all.

LEADER: And the government will be upon his shoulder, and his name will be called "Wonderful Counselor, Mighty God, Prince of Peace."

RESPONSE: God's grace has appeared for the salvation of all.

LEADER: Of the increase of his government and of peace there will be no end to establish it, and to uphold it with justice and with righteousness from this time forth and for evermore.

RESPONSE: God's grace has appeared for the salvation of all.
LEADER: Therefore live sober, upright, and godly lives.
RESPONSE: Awaiting our blessed hope, the appearing of the
         glory of our great God and Savior Jesus Christ.

Prayer of Dedication

Our lives abound with signs of your matchless love, O God. Our days are full because of your mercy. As those long ago journeyed to Bethlehem and felt great joy at what had occurred, so also we come before you, praising your name for what you have made known to us. Accept our tributes to the Christ-child; use them that he may grow in stature among all people.

Prayer of Thanksgiving

O Giver of every good and perfect gift, we come rejoicing at the birth of your Son, our Savior Jesus Christ. We give you thanks that your light shines forth in the world. You illuminate our darkness, drive away the clouds of gloom and despair; you send forth rays of hope to cheer us and warm us with the radiance of your redeeming love.

The carols we sing tell of your glory, how angels sang and shepherds watched as a star led them to behold your wonder. We give thanks for the amazement and wonder of your revelation, the many ways you surprise us, and visit us, and cause us to feel your presence. You can be found in the laughter and gaiety of noisy gatherings. On solemn occasions your majesty and strength evoke awe and praise.

The gifts we exchange are signs of your benevolence to us, how you came to earth and dwelt among us as Emmanuel, "God with us." The heavens are glad because of your presence, the earth rejoices with the peace you promise. The sea roars since you reign over it, and fields exult in praise of you. You have declared that you will not forsake your creation, and sealed your promise with the gift of a child. For that assurance, we thank you and offer you our gratitude forevermore.

The joy we feel reflects our blessed hope: the appearance in glory of our Savior Jesus Christ. We give thanks that Christ calls us to follow him and gives us the ministry of reconciliation to fulfill in his name. At this glorious time of his birth, help us to reach out to those who feel no joy, for whom thanksgiving is difficult because darkness enfolds them. Let us give to them a beacon of light that will lead them to your gift of new life.

FIRST SUNDAY AFTER CHRISTMAS

Lectionary Readings for the Day
Ps. 111; Isa. 61:10 to 62:3
Gal. 4:4–7; Luke 2:22–40

Seasonal Color:
White

Simeon, a righteous and devout old man blessed with the gift of God's Holy Spirit, meets Jesus, a child called "Emmanuel," full of promise for all God's people. Simeon sees salvation in the child, God's revelation that will bring light and glory to all who believe. Having held the child, Simeon may depart in peace. God's promise of eternal life remains for all who receive with open arms God's hope of salvation, Jesus of Nazareth.

Call to Worship
LEADER: Praise God. I will give thanks to God with my whole heart, in the company of the upright, in the congregation.
RESPONSE: God's work is full of honor and majesty, and God's righteousness endures for ever.
LEADER: Praise God in the sanctuary and remember the wonderful works God has done.
RESPONSE: God's praise endures for ever!

(Author's adaptation)

Prayer of Praise and Adoration
Eternal God of the covenant, you have clothed your people with the garments of salvation, and covered them with the robe of righteousness. We praise your name for your work of redemption, sending us Jesus as the promise of peace. Hear our rejoicing as we sing hymns of thanksgiving; hear our prayers as we give voice to our inmost thoughts. Fill us with the presence of your living Spirit, and give us wisdom to live in the light of your gifts.

Prayer of Confession
UNISON: God of compassion, have mercy upon us as we make our confession. The year is soon spent. What we ought to have done still awaits action, while we commit acts not in accord with your will. We think of ourselves before others; we serve our own needs. We keep for ourselves the gifts of your graciousness. The new life you offer is not yet proclaimed in the land. Forgive us our sins and make us more faithful. Help us to use our time wisely as we follow Christ's way.

Assurance of Pardon

LEADER: Hear Paul's words of assurance: "If we have died with Christ, we believe that we shall also live with him. . . . The death he died he died to sin, once for all, but the life he lives he lives to God. So you also must consider yourselves dead to sin and alive to God in Christ Jesus."* In Christ we are forgiven.

Prayer of Dedication

Eternal God of redemption, you bless your creation and it springs forth with beauty. You judge your people with righteousness and new life abounds. We bring you now the fruits of our labors. Bless the work of our hands, so that what we do reflects the radiance of your love. Fill us with your Holy Spirit, so that what we say proclaims to all people the new hope in Jesus.

Prayer of Thanksgiving and Intercession

Bringer of hope to the nations, glory be to you. We thank you that through the gift of your Son, Jesus, we can now be called heirs of your righteousness and children of the covenant. By your grace we bear the name Christ and are members of Christ's household of faith. We thank you for his call to ministry and for the empowerment of your Spirit, which enables us to respond.

We pray that our ministry may be more effective in the new year that awaits us. We thank you for watching over us in the days that have passed. Take the good that we have done, and by your grace increase it to the glory of your holy name. We are sorry for those actions of ours that have frustrated your design for creation. Forgive our failures, and keep us from compounding useless endeavors.

We pray for those we have overlooked for whatever reasons: the lonely, the sick, the maligned, the forgotten. Give us compassion to reach out to comfort them, and bestow in us a sense of your Holy Spirit, which can make them whole. Increase our vision to see clearly the causes of anger, hurt, and resentment, and where it is within our power to act, save us from hesitation.

We pray that nations may heed the word of peace that Christ proclaims. Be with all who suffer as a result of human hostility, and, through Christ, break down the walls that keep us apart. Fill leaders with wisdom; bring humility to rulers. Make us effective witnesses to the hope of Christ's salvation, and give us firm resolution to proclaim him Redeemer of all.

*Rom. 6:8, 10, 11.

We ask all this in the name of Jesus, who taught us to pray, Our Father...

29

a new

day

EPIPHANY

Lectionary Readings for the Day
Ps. 72:1–14; Isa. 60:1–6

Eph. 3:1–12; Matt. 2:1–12

Seasonal Color:
White

The heavens proclaim a birth in Bethlehem. Following a star, three Magi journey to see what has occurred. They carry with them gifts appropriate for a ruler: gold, frankincense, and myrrh. Upon arrival at the scene, they observe a mother and child, God's heavenly glory, on earth, to bring light to the nations. Proclaiming God's praise, they fall down and worship. The radiance of God's love evokes wonder and awe.

Call to Worship
LEADER: God comes to judge the people with righteousness, the poor with justice.

RESPONSE: The weak receive pity, and the needy are saved.

LEADER: Praise God for goodness, and give thanks for salvation.

(Author's adaptation)

RESPONSE: We worship God, who brings comfort and hope.

Prayer of Praise and Adoration
Merciful God of deliverance, we praise you for sending Jesus as Light for the nations. He is the glory and radiance of your compassion and care. Our eyes behold the brightness of your promised righteousness; you illumine our darkness with the hope of your justice. As generations before us, we stand in awe of your splendor; we bow down to worship you, lifting our voices in praise of your goodness and giving heed to your instruction.

Prayer of Confession
UNISON: Source of salvation and Bringer of light, we fail to sense the mystery of your love. We bear grudges against our neighbors, while it is your nature to forgive. We hold tightly to our possessions, while Christ blesses the poor. In him you have spoken peace, yet we live in turmoil. We care little for this planet, which you in goodness created for our habitation. In mercy forgive us, and help us to amend our ways.

Assurance of Pardon
LEADER: God is righteous and just, and forgives the iniquity of all who repent. Like "rain that falls on the mown grass, like

showers that water the earth," God's goodwill overflows toward us in the Babe of Bethlehem. Through that child, who is our risen Lord, we plead for forgiveness and claim mercy.

Prayer of Dedication

O God, as wise rulers of old brought gifts and worshiped a newly born baby, so also we bring offerings in praise of him whom you sent. The star that we follow is the light of Christ's teachings, calling us to be faithful in service to all in need. Accept what we earn, the products of our creative energy and talent. Let this be the gold, frankincense, and myrrh that we bring. By our gifts may a sad and needy world be enriched and comforted.

Prayer of Thanksgiving, Supplication, and Intercession

Eternal God of manifold wisdom, we give you thanks that through the gift of Jesus you have given us a glimpse into your plan for creation. He shows us how you rule the nations, bringing hope of justice to those in need, and deliverance to all captives. In him we see the promise of new life if only we follow his will for our lives.

Your infinite mercy is always before us, granting us haven from storm-tossed seas. We give you thanks that Jesus walked this earth, suffered more pain than we shall ever endure, and sits by your side to intercede for us. You know our needs before we voice them. Make your presence felt among us during our times of trial, and give us courage to face the suffering that will test our faith.

Let your all-encompassing presence be with those who, for whatever reasons, are in need of your loving care. Help them sense your healing power at work to ease their pain, shield them from the demonic powers of this world that seek to undermine their spirit, and protect them from any aggravation that might weaken them further.

We pray particularly for those in institutions who seem to be forgotten, those disturbed in mind and spirit. Bring wholeness to them, and a sense of your companionship in the midst of their loneliness. Let us not cast aside any who dwell among us, whether they be the simple, the slow, or the impaired. Rather, help us to see in them a special gleam of the light that Jesus brought to the world. We give you thanks for a righteousness that is all-inclusive, a hope that is ever sure, a deliverance that knows no limits, and a promise of life that is eternal, through Christ, whose going forth we celebrate today.

THE BAPTISM OF THE LORD
SUNDAY AFTER EPIPHANY

Lectionary Readings for the Day
Ps. 29; Gen. 1:1–5
Acts 19:1–7; Mark 1:4–11

Seasonal Color:
White

Jesus is baptized and proclaimed "beloved," chosen for a ministry that will condition his life. Full of God's Spirit, he will himself be tempted, but he will endure; he will call others to follow, and they will be led to obey; he will teach with wisdom that surpasses all earthly knowledge; he will perform acts of healing that reveal God's mercy. Christian ministry begins with baptism, which marks believers as God's chosen people.

Call to Worship
LEADER: Ascribe to God all glory and strength.
RESPONSE: We will ascribe to God the glory of God's name.
LEADER: Let us worship God in holy array.

(Author's adaptation)

Prayer of Praise and Adoration
You speak, O God, and the oceans tremble; their waters crest in waves that dash upon the shore. You speak and the heavens open; thunder signals the rains that freshen the earth. You breathe and the leaves shudder; the trees of the forest bow to your majesty. You speak and the Spirit descends on your people; we ascribe to you all glory as we worship your name.

Prayer of Confession
UNISON: We come as your baptized believers, O God, confessing our sins. You send forth your Spirit, yet we do not respond to your presence. You set us apart as water is poured over us, yet our behavior in faith does not match our unique status. Christ calls us to follow, yet we disobey his commandment. Evidence of your goodness surrounds us, yet we ignore your gracious ways. Have mercy upon us, and in your love uphold us. Above all, teach us the meaning of repentance.

Assurance of Pardon
LEADER: Hear the good news! God said to Jesus, "Thou art my beloved Son; with thee I am well pleased." We have a high priest who is able to sympathize with our weaknesses, who has been

tempted as we are, yet is without sin. In Christ's name we may draw near with confidence to the throne of grace, and there find mercy and grace to help in time of need.

Prayer of Dedication

Source of eternal renewal, we come before you full of new life. We hear Christ's call to follow, and seek to obey. We yearn to be faithful as his baptized believers. Accept these offerings as signs of our commitment, and use us to lead others to repentance. We pray in the name of him who calls us his own.

Prayer of Thanksgiving and Intercession

God of all creation, whose voice causes oceans to tremble, you lighten our darkness, give form to the void within, and send your Spirit as comfort and hope. We thank you for visiting us with mercy. Your goodness overwhelms us. We can look to you in times of need, rely on you to drive away our doubt, depend on your judgment to curb our folly, and live in the hope that one day Jesus shall reign.

There are those in our midst whose days are filled with uncertainty. Invade their gloom with the warmth of your loving care. Give them the sense that you are there. Lift them from feelings of futility, and enable them to grasp your abiding concern. Give us a measure of the compassion that Jesus showed. Help us to be open to all in need, that we may become instruments of your mercy.

We pray for those whose days lack luster, who wander aimlessly. Give to them a sense of your will for their lives, strength to pursue it, and the discipline to do what you would have them do. Erase from us our need to be critical of those who do not conform to our standards. Teach us forbearance as they seek to discern your intentions.

Make this day and all our days a celebration of our baptism. Fill us anew with your Spirit, and cleanse us of past sins, which estrange us from Christ and from one another. Send us forth as Christ's disciples, abounding in the hope of new life and proclaiming good news to aid the afflicted. Give us your blessing, O God of all creation.

SECOND SUNDAY AFTER EPIPHANY

Lectionary Readings for the Day

Ps. 63:1–8; I Sam. 3:1–10, (11–20)   *Seasonal Color:*

I Cor. 6:12–20; John 1:35–42   *Green*

The "Lamb of God" meets the "Rock" in today's Gospel lesson. Weakness and strength are parts of God's providence. The Lamb appears to be weak, but in the end becomes the source of our strength. The Rock seems to be strong but, when tested, reveals a weakness inherent in all Christ's followers. God's providence encompasses both our courage and our frailty; the Lamb of God remains the source of endurance.

Call to Worship

LEADER: O God, thou art my God, I seek thee, my soul thirsts for thee.

RESPONSE: So I have looked upon thee in the sanctuary, beholding thy power and glory.

LEADER: Because thy steadfast love is better than life, my lips will praise thee.

RESPONSE: So I will bless thee as long as I live; I will lift up my hands and call on thy name.

Prayer of Praise and Adoration

O God, you are our rock, the source of our strength; you are the fountainhead from which flow living waters. When our souls thirst after righteousness, your justice sustains us; in need of encouragement, we behold your power and glory. We lift our hands in the sanctuary; with our lips we praise you. We raise our voices in the company of believers and call on your name. Fill us now with your Holy Spirit, and nourish us by your presence.

Prayer of Confession

UNISON: O Lamb of God, who takes away the sin of the world, have mercy upon us as we make our confession. We grow lax in our discipline, and we disobey Christ. Our faith is flabby when put to the test; our courage vanishes in the face of temptation. Our joints stiffen when we are called to act. We profess loyalty, while our bodies deny commitment. Have mercy upon us and forgive us.

Assurance of Pardon

LEADER: Hear Paul's words when he writes: "Do you not know that your body is a temple of the Holy Spirit within you, which you have from God? You are not your own; you were bought with a price." Christ mercifully paid the price for our sin. Through him we may approach God with our temples made clean.

Prayer of Dedication

O God, you nourish us by the outpouring of your love. You strengthen us with your enlivening Spirit. Our bodies are sustained by your goodness and power. You are the source of every good act we perform and of every talent we possess. These gifts are but a portion of what you give us in abundance. Accept them as signs of our thanksgiving.

Prayer of Thanksgiving and Intercession

Incarnate Word of life, eternal, unchanging, you call us to discipleship, and we seek to follow. Your will surpasses all earthly wisdom; you are known to us amid our dreams and our deliberations. Sleeping or waking, we cannot hide from your presence. You are around us and within us; you direct us and watch over us. We give you thanks for your incarnate grace.

Soften those who resist your truth. Surprise them with the message of new life that awaits their response. Turn them from making themselves their only source of value, and show them how your mercy can transform their worth.

Surround and nourish the young in faith, the newly baptized, whose commitment has not been tested. Keep them from trials beyond their capacity to endure, yet help them take risks that will strengthen their resolve to stand firm in Jesus Christ. Build up their confidence through the gift of your Holy Spirit. Enable us in the family of faith to be a source of assurance and support to them.

Startle those who have grown complacent, whose commitment to Christ has become a leisure-time activity. Intrude in our lives with the transforming revelation of your judgment, and astonish us with a sense of your awesome power. Keep us from seeking comforts above discipleship, and make of us faithful witnesses to your eternal and incarnate Word.

Lectionary Readings for the Day
 Ps. 62:5–12; Jonah 3:1–5, 10
 I Cor. 7:29–31, (32–35); Mark 1:14–20

Seasonal Color:
Green

Jesus calls the disciples to follow. No bargaining occurs; conditions are not discussed; there isn't even much time given to decide. Mark's Gospel makes the whole episode quite matter-of-fact. To follow Jesus is both a command and a promise. The command involves forsaking one's past in an act of obedience. The promise implies that as one makes the decision, the future will be revealed. The disciples immediately leave their nets and follow.

Call to Worship
 LEADER: For God alone my soul waits in silence, for my hope is from God.
 RESPONSE: God only is my rock and my salvation; I shall not be shaken.
 LEADER: Trust in God at all times, O people; pour out your heart before God.
 RESPONSE: Our trust is in God. We worship God's name.

Prayer of Praise and Adoration
 You are our rock and our strength, O God, and in you rests our deliverance. You defend us in the midst of adversity; you protect us from ultimate harm. You humble the mighty with acts that manifest your transcendent power; the lowly you comfort with your tender embrace. We gather this day, saved by your mercy. Hear now our praises as we herald your greatness.

Prayer of Confession
 UNISON: God of compassion and mercy, hear us as we make our confession. Christ preaches repentance; we do not heed his call. Your new day is proclaimed; we dwell on the past. We turn not from our evil ways, nor do we sacrifice those treasures that give us status. We say we obey you, but our deeds betray us. By your grace renew us, and cleanse us of sin.

Assurance of Pardon
 LEADER: Hear the good news: "The time is fulfilled, and the kingdom of God is at hand; repent, and believe in the gospel."

God is merciful and just, and in Jesus Christ promises redemption to all who believe. As we turn from our old ways and respond with faith to Christ's call, we receive the assurance that we shall be saved.

Prayer of Dedication

Eternal Source of refuge and trust, our days are filled with your abiding presence. We awaken with the dawn of new life. We labor with assurance that you bless the work of our hands. We sleep at peace in the promise of your protection and care. All that we are and all that we do are signs of your benevolent deliverance. Accept now the gifts we bring you as tokens of our unending devotion.

Prayer of Thanksgiving and Supplication

O God of Jonah, of Jesus, of Paul and the disciples, throughout the ages you have called your people to repentance. We give you thanks for your saving grace shown to Nineveh, that your wrath was withheld because of their repentance. We give you thanks for the promise of Jesus, that those who turn from their evil ways and follow him are assured of life anew. We give you thanks for all the disciples who testified to your faithfulness. In spite of their trials, they persevered, and left us a legacy of what it means to repent.

Have mercy upon us as we join this host of witnesses. Save us from your anger as we turn to you with contrite hearts, imploring your forgiveness. You know our inmost thoughts, hidden desires, and everything we do in betraying your will. We rely on your goodness to overcome our weakness, and your endless mercy to redeem us from sin.

Strengthen within us the resolve to be faithful. Give us the needed discipline to let go of old forms of security and to risk putting our trust in your will. As we take our first few halting steps of faith, encourage us with the vision of your reign on earth. Lift us from a sense of defeat when we stumble and fall.

Make of us, O God of deliverance, beacons of light to show others the way. By our examples of faithfulness, bring them to a greater sense of your justice and righteousness. By our claims of obedience, lead them to be willing to practice their faith. Support us with your Holy Spirit as we surround them with our care and concern. Help us make a fresh witness to your saving grace.

FOURTH SUNDAY AFTER EPIPHANY

Lectionary Readings for the Day
Ps. 111; Deut. 18:15–20
I Cor. 8:1–13; Mark 1:21–28

Seasonal Color:
Green

The authority of Jesus is cause for amazement. His teachings are not what the people expected. Even demons obey him; their power is dissolved. The crowds are astonished by what he accomplishes. God's order has a way of upsetting the prevailing state of affairs. What is taught provides a new vision of what ought to be. What is done testifies to the unlimited scope of God's goodness and love.

Call to Worship
LEADER: God be praised!
RESPONSE: I will give thanks to God with my whole heart, in the company of the upright, in the congregation.
LEADER: The fear of God is the beginning of wisdom. A good understanding have all those who practice it.
RESPONSE: God's praise endures for ever!

(Author's adaptation)

Prayer of Praise and Adoration
Great God of the universe, whose wisdom pervades all creation, we gather before you to give you all praise and honor. Wonderful and majestic are your works; righteousness is seen in all that you do. You make a covenant and call us as heirs of its promise. You establish your law, showing all people that you are to be trusted. In company with the redeemed of all ages, we lift our voices to acclaim your worth.

Prayer of Confession
UNISON: God of mercy, show compassion as we make our confession. You command us to tell of your mighty deeds, yet we remain silent. You call us to act faithfully, yet we are slow to respond. We claim to be wise, but we know not your law. Our allegiance is divided, for we worship false gods. Help us to obey Christ, to whom we owe our existence, and to love our neighbors, whom we are commanded to serve.

Assurance of Pardon
LEADER: Paul reminds us, "There is one God, . . . from whom are all things and for whom we exist, and one Lord, Jesus Christ,

through whom are all things and through whom we exist. . . . If one loves God, one is known by God." As we confess our sin before God, God is faithful and just, and in Jesus Christ, through whom we exist, God forgives us our sin.

Prayer of Dedication

Most merciful and gracious God, the good that we do we owe to your righteousness. Whatever honor we receive is due to your redeeming love in Christ Jesus. All that we have is a gift of your grace. You call us, you name us, you watch over us with care. We bring now our gifts in response to your goodness. Use them and us to further the work of your eternal benevolence, through Jesus Christ, whom we seek to obey.

Prayer of Thanksgiving and Intercession

O Holy One, whose righteousness endures forever, we give you thanks for the prophets who faithfully spoke your word. We give you thanks for Jesus Christ, who obediently performed acts of mercy on behalf of those who suffered. We give you thanks for the apostle Paul, who taught what it means to take into account the needs of others. Through Christ, who intercedes when our words are not adequate, hear our prayer as we speak on behalf of those who concern us.

We pray for those in the thrall of false gods. Give to them a sense of your majesty that cannot be limited, your wonder that spans the universe, your goodness that cares for even the smallest creature of nature, your comforting Spirit that hears the faintest cry. Let them find no satisfaction in their closets full of goods that wear out with age. Lead them to your Word that endures through the ages, even Jesus Christ, who makes known your merciful deeds.

We pray for those the world calls wise. Give them a sense of humility, and grant them perspective to accompany their vision. May they not mistake power for justice or order for well-being. When they are called upon to make decisions, hold them particularly close to you and make them instruments of your peace.

Give to the weak a sense of your blessing, and help us support them in their search for life's meaning. Let us see them as partners in this venture of faithfulness, and together help us grow closer to righteousness, in Jesus Christ, who endures forever.

Lectionary Readings for the Day

Ps. 147:1–11; Job 7:1–7
I Cor. 9:16–23; Mark 1:29–39

Seasonal Color:
Green

The compassion of Jesus has a healing effect! The crowds bring to him those who are sick and possessed. He lays his hands on them, comforts them, lifts them out of their misery, and heals them. Throughout his ministry, he remains aware of the source of his healing power, for he will withdraw and be in prayer with God. Compassion, healing, and being at one with God are marks of Jesus' ministry.

Call to Worship

LEADER: Praise God! For it is good to sing praises to our God; for God is gracious, and a song of praise is seemly.
RESPONSE: God is great, and abundant in power; God's understanding is beyond measure.
LEADER: Sing to God with thanksgiving; make melody to our God upon the lyre!
RESPONSE: We sing praises to God as we worship God's name.

Prayer of Praise and Adoration

Great God of the universe, you set the stars on course in the heavens; the earth radiates your glory and honor. The rain never falls without your knowing it; the fields produce their harvest according to your design. We admire the strength by which you rule the nations; we bow down in adoration at how you care for your children. We gather gladly to herald your encompassing acts of goodwill. Hear us as we respond by giving you praise.

Prayer of Confession

UNISON: O God, you heal the brokenhearted; save us from sin when we inflict pain on our neighbors. We bear grudges against those who deceive us. We seek revenge on those who hurt us. Some we judge inferior, since they don't meet our standards. Others we deem unworthy of our respect and support. Jesus had compassion upon all who were afflicted. Forgive us, O God, when our hearts are hardened against neighbors in need.

Assurance of Pardon

LEADER: The assurance of our pardon resides in Christ, "who, though he was in the form of God, . . . emptied himself, taking the form of a servant."* Today, he intercedes on behalf of human weakness before the great throne of God. Therefore, let every knee bow, and let every tongue confess that Jesus Christ is Lord. Therein lies our assurance that we are forgiven!

Prayer of Dedication

You are worthy, O God, of more honor than mere humans can hope to bestow on you. You are God of all creation, and the source of all goodness. We dare to approach you with our gifts of thanksgiving. Receive them as symbols of our wholehearted praise. Transform what we bring you to harmonize with your wishes, and convert all our actions according to your will.

Prayer of Thanksgiving and Intercession

O God of sympathy and tenderness, who surrounded Job when he was despondent and sent Jesus to bind the wounds of the afflicted, we give you thanks that you take pity upon us and nurse us to wholeness when we are distressed and forlorn. We give you thanks that even when despair so easily overtakes us, you send your Spirit to comfort our fears.

Hear us as we pray for those confined by illness. In the midst of their infirmities, help them to sense your healing presence, which brings peace of mind. Give to them that patience which allows their bodies to draw upon those sources of regeneration so necessary to health and vigor. When the days are full of fretting, and nights prolong the anxiety over a new dawn of suffering, hold them in your bosom and grant them peace.

Hear us as we pray for those who despair. When earthly hope seems to elude them, grant them a vision of your boundless mercy. Appear to them in the sadness of their darkest moments, and make real for them the victory of Christ's resurrection. Help them to hear the good news that transforms light out of darkness, and may they henceforth have confidence in your loving care.

Hear us as we pray for those blessed with sound minds and well bodies. Help them to care for those temples of your grace. Keep them from abusing what you so intricately created, and give them discipline to look after themselves. We give you thanks for the countless mercies we take for granted: for movement, for strength, for our minds and our senses. Help us, O God, to take heed of our health as a gift freely given, and never cease to praise you for the grace it reflects.

*Phil. 2:6, 7.

Lectionary Readings for the Day

Ps. 32; II Kings 5:1–14

I Cor. 9:24–27; Mark 1:40–45

Seasonal Color:
Green

Jesus seeks obedience in response to his ministry. He shows genuine compassion for people; he cares for them, cleansing them of their infirmities. Yet he does not want to be known only as a worker of miracles, so he teaches those he heals to give God the glory, and faithfully to follow God's commands. But the people are thinking more about what Jesus can do for them than about what they can do for him.

Call to Worship

LEADER: Be glad in your Redeemer, and rejoice, O righteous.

RESPONSE: Shout for joy, you upright in heart!

(Author's adaptation)

LEADER: Let us worship God.

Prayer of Praise and Adoration

Eternal God, we come rejoicing with gladness of heart, singing your praises and adoring your wondrous gifts of love. You cause the darkness of night to steal away with the dawn. You bring us promise of new life in the gift of Jesus our Savior. We arise refreshed from the rest you give, and wait for your Spirit to fill us with the hope of the gospel. Come, Creator Spirit, and dwell here among us. Hear our songs of thanksgiving as we seek to worship you in thought, word, and deed.

Prayer of Confession

UNISON: Merciful God, hear our confession as we pray in Christ's name. We claim to be faithful, but we obey not your commandments. We boast of our hope, yet we dwell not in faith. We gather security about us while others go hungry. We arm ourselves mightily as though we could buy peace of mind. We hear Christ's words of assurance, but we live not in his promise. Forgive our ambivalence, as in Christ we repent.

Assurance of Pardon

LEADER: Our help is in God. "It is God who justifies. . . . Is it Christ Jesus, who died, yes, who was raised from the dead, who is at the right hand of God, who indeed intercedes for us? Who shall separate us from the love of Christ?"* Know that as we confess our sin, God is just. Through Jesus Christ, who intercedes on our behalf, we have assurance that God forgives us.

Prayer of Dedication

God of all grace and goodness, throughout the ages you have looked after the needs of your children; we thank you for your mercy. Bless the words we speak, that they may proclaim your greatness. Look with favor on those acts we perform, that we may show others your tender love. Make us responsive to the high calling of Jesus, as we offer you gifts in his name.

Prayer of Thanksgiving and Supplication

God of healing and wholeness, we give thanks for the prophets, who proclaimed your power to cleanse the afflicted and restore them to health. We give you thanks for our Savior, the Christ, whose touch cured those in need. We give thanks for Paul's vision of what it means to obey you. Help us, we pray, to run the race of faith, that we may seize the goal of our calling, and obtain the prize of deliverance Christ promises to all.

We pray that you will renew our drooping spirits and give us fresh hope. Sustain our confidence during those times of trial that encroach on our sense of well-being. Keep us from submitting to temptation, and uphold us with your commandments, which show us your will. When our energy wanes, or we lack the discipline to press on with commitment, enthuse us and enliven us through the gift of your Holy Spirit.

We pray that you will restore in us a new sense of the gospel. Help us regain the excitement of when we first came to have faith. Let the teachings of the Scripture sound afresh to our listening ears, and help us recall those initial confessions we made to follow the Christ. As we remember our baptism, strengthen our resolve to live in the light of your cleansing pardon, alive to the dawn of your redeeming grace.

We pray that you will remake us in the image of those prophets, apostles, and disciples who gave their lives in utmost devotion. Make of us witnesses of what it means to believe. Keep us from being satisfied with our current level of devotion, consigned to the present as though our response were sufficient. Rather, like Paul, urge us to run the good race with unflagging zeal, aiming to please you in all that we do.

*Rom. 8:33–35.

SEVENTH SUNDAY AFTER EPIPHANY

Lectionary Readings for the Day
Ps. 41; Isa. 43:18–25

II Cor. 1:18–22; Mark 2:1–12

Seasonal Color:
Green

Jesus forgives sins and alarms the authorities. The scribes think it blasphemy to forgive sins. The friends of the paralytic have faith that Jesus can heal him. The crowds are amazed and give God the glory. Similar scenarios will be repeated throughout the ministry of Jesus. As Jesus proclaims God's will, many will question his authority, some will have faith. In the end, God will be glorified.

Call to Worship
LEADER: All the promises of God find their Yes in Christ.

RESPONSE: That is why we utter the Amen through him, to the glory of God.

LEADER: But it is God who establishes us with you in Christ, and has commissioned us.

RESPONSE: God has put God's seal upon us and given us God's Spirit in our hearts as a guarantee.

LEADER: Let us worship God.

Prayer of Praise and Adoration
God of promise and fulfillment, hear our resounding "Amen" to your glorious deeds. You caused Christ to come to earth as our redeemer and the giver of new life. You sent forth your Holy Spirit to guide us with counsel and might. You commissioned us as your people, sealed by your covenant and empowered by your grace. We laud your manifold deeds of mercy, and say "Amen" to the glory of your holy name.

Prayer of Confession
UNISON: Eternal God, have mercy upon us, for we burden you with our sins. We do not bring you our offerings; we seldom make sacrifices. Praise of your glory is not often heard; we are dedicated to seeking our own fortunes. We live not by faith but by our own resources. Forgive our reluctance to accept your promises, forgive our human quest for security at all costs, and help us to commit our lives to you alone.

Assurance of Pardon

LEADER: Hear the words of assurance as the prophet Isaiah records them: "Remember not the former things, nor consider the things of old. Behold, I am doing a new thing; now it springs forth, do you not perceive it? I will make a way in the wilderness and rivers in the desert. . . . I, I am God who blots out your transgressions for my own sake, and I will not remember your sins." In Christ, God remains faithful and forgives us our sins.

Prayer of Dedication

Eternal God of the covenant, you call us, commission us, and fill us with your Holy Spirit. We gather as Christ's people in response to your call. We seek to be faithful to your commission to make disciples of all nations. Filled with your Spirit, our hearts beat with joy as with our voices we sing praises to you. You are the God of our faith, just, true, and righteous. Accept now our offerings in response to your love.

Prayer of Thanksgiving

Merciful God, it is good to give thanks for your manifold gifts of love. For gracious acts shown in countless ways, we praise your name. We stand in line with generations who have gone before, as we consider your blessings to us. You called us as those worthy to bear the name of your chosen people. You included us within the boundless love of your covenant, and saw fit to seal our eternal future in the person of Christ. He bore our sins on the cross. We give thanks that you remove our transgressions for his sake.

We give you thanks that he intercedes on our behalf. In Christ we know that you stoop to hear the cries of the suffering; you comfort the lonely, and the needy you send not away. We are grateful that all manner of human want is within the embrace of your encompassing care for all of creation. We can dwell in peace, since you are faithful and you forget not your own.

We give you thanks that you send forth your Spirit to dwell amid the frenzied pace of our daily lives. As the paralytic was lowered through the roof to face Jesus, so we descend through the barriers of our defenses to confront your healing presence. Enabled by the indwelling gift of your redeeming forgiveness, we can confidently face whatever challenges await us.

Help us count each day an occasion to greet you with our songs of thanksgiving. Grant that we may number each hour a moment to be filled with praise of your name. We give thanks to you for your countless gifts of love.

EIGHTH SUNDAY AFTER EPIPHANY

Lectionary Readings for the Day
Ps. 103:1–13; Hos. 2:14–20
II Cor. 3:1–6; Mark 2:18–22

Seasonal Color:
Green

There is talk of a new day. Prior perceptions will no longer be adequate; old forms will not be suitable; past practices will no longer suffice. Jesus prepares his followers for what is to come. The bridegroom dwells among them and is no longer awaited. They are to be filled with the new wine of the gospel. They are to put on the cloth of righteousness and greet the new day!

Call to Worship
LEADER: Praise God, O my soul; and all that is within me, bless God's holy name!
RESPONSE: Praise God, O my soul, and forget not all God's benefits.

(Author's adaptation)

LEADER: Let us worship God.

Prayer of Praise and Adoration
Holy God, merciful and gracious, slow to anger, and abounding in steadfast love, we greet you with praise on our lips and thanksgiving in our hearts. You take pity upon us and shower us with your blessings, satisfying our every need and renewing our strength. You lift us above all earthly cares, and grant us a vision of your eternal salvation. We bow in reverence before you and rise to praise you. You are the God of new life.

Litany of Confession
LEADER: I will remove the names of Baals from your mouths.
RESPONSE: Forgive us, O God, for we worship false gods.
LEADER: I will make for you a covenant with the beasts of the field, the birds of the air, and the creeping things of the ground.
RESPONSE: Forgive us, O God, when we despise your creation.
LEADER: I will abolish war, and make you lie down in safety.
RESPONSE: Forgive us, O God, since we do not seek peace.
LEADER: I will betroth you to me in righteousness.
RESPONSE: Forgive us, O God, for we love not our neighbor.
LEADER: I will betroth you to me in faithfulness, and you shall know the God of Israel.
RESPONSE: Forgive us our sin, O God, and grant us your pardon.

(Author's adaptation)

Assurance of Pardon

LEADER: "God is merciful and gracious, slow to anger and abounding in steadfast love. God will not always chide; God's anger does not last for ever. God does not deal with us according to our sins, nor requite us according to our iniquities." I tell you, in Jesus Christ we are forgiven!

Prayer of Dedication

O God of new life, you restore us with the hope of the gospel; you bind up our wounds and make us whole once again. You enliven us with the gift of your Spirit. Accept the gifts we bring, and transform their worth to accord with your will.

Prayer of Thanksgiving and Supplication

O God, in Christ Jesus you have written the new covenant indelibly upon the hearts of humankind; we give you thanks for your grace, mercy, and favor. You do not hold our sins against us, but deal with us as a loving parent who bears with rebellious and errant children. You withhold not your love, but continually shower us with blessings beyond our hopes and desires. Your patience extends beyond the farthest reaches of the horizon; your care probes the very depths of creation. You are God of the great beyond and the immediate moment, of the unknown future and the recorded past. There is nowhere we can go to escape your dominion. We give you thanks that you have seen fit to crown us with your glory and in Christ call us your own.

Renew these earthen vessels we call our bodies. Enable us to become fit receptacles for the new life in the Spirit. When cracks appear from the countless pressures upon us, keep us from being content with just mending the tear. When our energies wane because of overcommitment, or conflict saps our strength to pursue peaceful negotiations, keep us from relying upon worn-out solutions.

Make us worthy to carry the banner of your redeeming grace to all people here on earth. Invest us with the truth of Christ's reconciling love, so that we become instruments of your peace rather than weapons of hostility. Awaken within us the contagion of forgiveness, so that we can henceforth act out your justice and dwell in your mercy. Through Christ we pray.

LAST SUNDAY AFTER EPIPHANY
TRANSFIGURATION

Lectionary Readings for the Day
Ps. 50:1–6; II Kings 2:1–12a
II Cor. 4:3–6; Mark 9:2–9

Seasonal Color:
White

Jesus leads his three disciples up a high mountain and there is transfigured before them. The light of the gospel will henceforth shine on the darkness of the world. A cloud appears, and they hear a voice proclaim, "This is my beloved Son; listen to him." No longer can anything on earth or in heaven separate God's people from the love Christ came to reveal. The glory of Christ shone in order that God's will would be known.

Call to Worship
LEADER: The Mighty One speaks and summons the earth from the rising of the sun to its setting.
RESPONSE: Keep not your silence before us, O God, but let the heavens declare your righteousness, for you alone can judge us.

(Author's adaptation)

LEADER: Let us worship God.

Prayer of Praise and Adoration
Morning by morning you awaken us, O God; day by day you show us your wondrous love. The words of your commandments fall fresh upon our listening ears; we heed your wisdom and are renewed by your word. You surround us with countless acts that tell of your majesty; we are struck by your goodness as we are refreshed in your Spirit. Come, dwell among us, and through Christ let us praise you. You are the God whom we worship and adore.

Prayer of Confession
UNISON: God of compassion, have mercy upon us as we confess our sin. In Christ you bring light, yet we still dwell in darkness. Your word offers guidance, but we choose to ignore your counsel. You promise renewal, but we heed not your wisdom. We bow to the gods of this world, choosing to hide from your truth. Speak to us again from beyond the clouds of our sinfulness; dazzle us anew with the light of Christ's love. Restore and forgive us.

Assurance of Pardon

LEADER: Hear the good news. God is light, and in God there is no darkness. "If we say we have fellowship with God while we walk in darkness, we lie and do not live according to the truth; but if we walk in the light, as God is in the light, we have fellowship with one another, and the blood of Jesus, God's Son, cleanses us from all sin." God is faithful and just, and Jesus Christ forgives us our sin.

Prayer of Dedication

O God, you hide not your radiance, neither hold back your word. You come to us in love, fresh as the morning. We are sustained by your mercy and renewed through your grace. You have sent us your Spirit to freshen our day. All that we are we owe to you. Accept our gifts and bless our endeavors, so that all we do may accord with your will.

Prayer of Thanksgiving and Supplication

Great Source of light, wisdom, and truth, you make all things new by the radiance of your transforming love. We give thanks for the Christ who leads us to the mountain and there sets before us your plan for creation. We give thanks that you speak from behind the clouds that surround us, sending forth hope that we may travel your path of new life. We give you thanks for your Spirit who dwells among us, encouraging us to follow your call for justice and peace.

Continue to enlighten us with your word, that we may ever be faithful to what you would have us be and do. Dispel the shadows of doubt that hover in spite of Christ's intercession on our behalf. In the face of conflict, we shrink from standing firm in the truth. Confronted with the pain of those who suffer, we lack confidence in our ability to comfort them. Envelop us in the truth that you can do all things through those who believe in you.

Spread your wisdom abroad in a land whose leaders so often lack direction. We speak of peace while the thunder of war is heard in distant corners of the earth. You command us to love neighbors, but we are prisoners of self-interest and greed. Pleas for justice fall on deaf ears. Bring order to our chaos, O God, and restore us through a vision of your care for all.

As we descend the mountain, accompany us on our journey of faithfulness. In the wilderness, help us to know that you will not forsake us. In the city's streets, direct us to the needy. Show us that wherever we go you are with us.

Spirit

and in the

truth of new life

FIRST SUNDAY IN LENT

Lectionary Readings for the Day

Ps. 25:1–10; Gen. 9:8–17

I Peter 3:18–22; Mark 1:9–15

Seasonal Color:
Violet

A trilogy of dramatic events in Mark's Gospel involves Jesus' baptism by John, his testing in the wilderness, and his preaching the gospel. Each event is significant because of what it implies for us: Those who follow Jesus will be cleansed of their past. They will be filled with the Holy Spirit, and sustained when put to the test. They will dwell in God's time, a time of new life. The message rings clearly: Repent and believe; God's reign is at hand!

Call to Worship

LEADER: To thee, O God, I lift up my soul. O my God, in thee I trust.

RESPONSE: Make me to know thy ways, O God; teach me thy paths.

LEADER: Let us worship God.

Prayer of Praise and Adoration

Your paths are straight and true, O God; they guide all who seek the way of salvation. By your mercy you instruct your children how to pursue steadfast love and faithfulness. Upheld by your covenant and enlightened by your testimony, we live securely in your goodness and truth. Hear us now as we lift our souls in praise to you. Accept our glad adoration, and teach us your will.

Prayer of Confession

UNISON: Have mercy upon us and hear our prayer, O God. We have failed to live in the light of your covenant. You set your rainbow above us, yet clouds of unbelief darken our days. Distrust wells within us; fear, not hope, is our watchword. Your Beloved bids us follow, but we are slow to obey. Without your grace, we are fruitless and inert. In mercy renew us and bring us to life, through Jesus Christ.

Assurance of Pardon

LEADER: Remember that Christ died for sins once and for all, that he might bring us to God cleansed of unrighteousness. "Baptism . . . now saves you, not as a removal of dirt from the body but as an appeal to God for a clear conscience, through the resurrection of Jesus Christ." Remember your baptism and live in new life, assured of forgiveness through Christ, who intercedes on our behalf.

Prayer of Dedication
God of our hope and salvation, your covenant names us, your grace sustains us. Your Chosen One calls us, and in our baptism sets us apart. We are a people called to minister, and equipped through your mercy to perform deeds of compassion and love. Accept our offerings as tokens of our faithfulness; enhance their effectiveness in accordance with your will. May all that we do be a clear sign of our willingness to respond to the call of Christ.

Prayer of Thanksgiving and Supplication
O God of the covenant, who turned the waters from a cause of death to a source of life, we praise you for our baptism received in Christ's name. We give thanks that through him you saw fit to set us apart for ministry. You gave us the rainbow as a sign of your covenant, an everlasting promise that you will never separate yourself from us. You have given your Spirit to rest upon us and dwell within us, so that we are empowered for service. Truly, in you we live, and move, and have our being. You are the Alpha and the Omega, the beginning and the end of our existence. By you alone are we sustained and upheld.

Continue to make your presence known as we face the barren times of life. Help us to see in the creation the manifold signs of your care for us. Instill within us confidence to trust in you, courage to face the powers that threaten us, and boldness to praise your name despite all difficulty. Set your covenant rainbow above us as the sign of your faithfulness, and beyond us as the beckoning light of your righteous love.

When Christ bids us come, give us strength to forsake all earthly ties and follow him. Help us to catch the vision of what you would have us do; give us signs of assurance that assist us to obey. Frustrate our efforts when we are headstrong and ignorant. Keep us faithful to our baptism and open to the leading of your Spirit, as fit recipients of your covenant. In grace sustain us as we respond.

SECOND SUNDAY IN LENT

Lectionary Readings for the Day
Ps. 105:1–11; Gen. 17:1–10, 15–19
Rom. 4:16–25; Mark 8:31–38

Seasonal Color:
Violet

Peter is rebuked because he misunderstood what it meant to follow Jesus. Jesus must suffer, even be put to death. To be his disciple means sacrifice as well. Such a thought was difficult for Peter, just as it is for us today. To lose one's life for Christ's sake is to put self behind and serve others without thought of reward.

Call to Worship
LEADER: O give thanks to God, call on God's name, make known God's deeds among the peoples!
RESPONSE: Sing to God, sing praises to God, tell of all God's wonderful works!
LEADER: Glory in God's holy name. Let us worship God.

Prayer of Praise and Adoration
We glory in your holy name, O God; we marvel at your wondrous works. You gathered a nation around you and called it blessed. You spared not your own Son, but sent him in the midst of a people to redeem them from sin. We gather this day to bear witness to your majesty. Our hearts rejoice in the promise of your covenant of love; our souls are cleansed by your mercy. Our bodies rise to bless your name; our voices sing your praises.

Prayer of Confession
UNISON: God of compassion and mercy, look with favor upon us as we confess our sins. Our faith is weak in the face of crisis. Our hope collapses when we are threatened or maligned. We seek our own safety and abandon those you love. We trust in objects we can create and control. We speak much and risk little. But you, O God, have given your promise that you will never forsake us. Forgive our failure to take you at your word.

Assurance of Pardon
LEADER: God's promises rest on grace and are guaranteed to all who believe in Christ. "I will establish my covenant between me and you and your descendants after you throughout their generations." "Faith will be reckoned as righteousness to us who believe in the One who raised Jesus our Lord, who was put to death for

our trespasses and raised for our justification." Trust the promises of grace, and accept the righteousness of God bestowed in Christ.

Prayer of Dedication

Source of all goodness, what can we give that has not already been given to us? Surely no gift of ours can repay Christ's gift of love. Therefore we offer ourselves, with thanksgiving for new life in the Spirit, and place before you what we have in response to your love. Use us in ways that fulfill your plan for creation, and bless what we give, so that others may learn of your ways.

Prayer of Thanksgiving

Gracious God, whom we trust in childlike faith, we give you thanks for setting apart Abraham and Sarah as parents in faith. We draw courage from their example of obedience. From them we gain confidence that you will never forsake us. What to us is beyond belief, in you becomes possible, O God. We trust the promise and await your call to pilgrimage.

We thank you for Jesus, who taught what it means to be obedient unto death. In his earthly ministry, he showed the way of discipleship; we are heirs of his words and example. We give thanks that you have revealed your wisdom and continue to involve us in your reign of righteousness and truth. Christ's faith abides forever as our means of deliverance. We walk in the light of your judgment, ever thankful for the living Word.

We praise you for the Holy Spirit, who sustains us amid doubts and trials. When earthly pressures weigh upon us and we are near despair, your Spirit brings release, giving encouragement to lighten our burden. You alone are the assurance that strengthens, the light that illuminates, the truth that dispels disbelief. You are the source of all hope, O God of the covenant. We can endure if you abide with us as you have promised.

You are indeed a God for all seasons. We give you thanks that you see fit to look with favor on us in this time and place. For Christ who nourishes and the Spirit who sustains, we give you all praise and bless your name!

THIRD SUNDAY IN LENT

Lectionary Readings for the Day
Ps. 19:7–14; Ex. 20:1–17

I Cor. 1:22–25; John 2:13–22

Seasonal Color:
Violet

The tables are turned on the money changers! Jesus was angered by their disregard for the Temple; God's house was never intended to be merely a trading place. However, more than the tables get turned, for in his prophecy Jesus predicts how true worship will occur. He points to his resurrection, when believers will worship him in spirit and in the truth of new life. No longer will God's praise be confined to some building.

Call to Worship
LEADER: Remember the sabbath day, to keep it holy.

RESPONSE: Let the words of my mouth and the meditation of my heart be acceptable in thy sight, my Rock and my Redeemer.

LEADER: Let us worship God.

Prayer of Praise and Adoration
O Holy One of Israel, in Christ you call us to dwell in your favor; we gather to praise you and worship your name. You are the rock that keeps us from falling, the redeemer who can save us from sin. You set us upon the sure foundation of your commandments; you cleanse us from all unrighteousness through the gift of your Son. Accept our words as we honor your judgment, and be pleased with our worship as we respond to Christ's call.

Litany of Confession
LEADER: God's law is perfect; it revives the soul.

RESPONSE: Forgive us, O God, for we obey not your commandments.

LEADER: God's testimony is sure; it makes wise the simple.

RESPONSE: Forgive us, O God, for we place status above service.

LEADER: God's precepts are right; they rejoice the heart.

RESPONSE: Forgive us, O God, for we take delight in false gods.

LEADER: God's commandment is pure; it enlightens the eyes.

RESPONSE: Forgive us, O God, for we overlook our neighbor's needs.

LEADER: God's ordinances are true; they are altogether righteous.

(Author's adaptation)

RESPONSE: O God, have mercy upon us; only you can save us. In Christ redeem us and cleanse us of sin.

Assurance of Pardon

LEADER: Our assurance is this: "There is therefore now no condemnation for those who are in Christ Jesus. . . . For God has done what the law, weakened by the flesh, could not do." God sent the Savior, who redeems us of all unworthiness.

Prayer of Dedication

O God of justice and mercy, your way commands our obedience, your grace gives us encouragement. We can do nothing apart from the blessings you bestow. Alive with the presence of your indwelling Spirit, we are bold to offer what we have as signs of our devotion. Accept what we bring, and multiply its effectiveness, for the sake of Jesus, your gift to us.

Prayer of Thanksgiving and Supplication

Eternal Source of guidance and direction, what you require you also reveal, and what you ask of us you also enable. There is nothing good that we do apart from your making it possible; you are the source and the finisher of our faith. We give thanks for Christ Jesus, who fulfills on our behalf all that you could possibly want us to be. We give thanks for Scripture, which sets forth your will and way for your chosen people. We give thanks for the Holy Spirit, who encourages us in every way.

We pray that our worship may be in accordance with the spirit and the truth of our new life in Christ. Hear us this day as we give thanks for countless blessings from your hand. When we awake, remind us of Christ's resurrection. As we gather for worship, hear our intercessions on behalf of others, and strengthen us to serve them in appropriate ways. Help us to draw apart for moments of quiet and rest during the day. Discipline us to recall how Christ spent time alone, refreshing himself through meditation and prayer. When evening comes and the shadows lengthen, make us mindful of your sustaining grace.

With your Spirit to guide us, and our worship rehearsing for us how you are never far from us, help us become the disciples Christ would have us be. Attune our lives to the intent of your commandments, that we may come to love you with soul, mind, and body and be enabled to love our neighbors as ourselves. We pray in the name of Jesus, who makes possible such love.

FOURTH SUNDAY IN LENT

Lectionary Readings for the Day
Ps. 137:1–6; II Chron. 36:14–23
Eph. 2:4–10; John 3:14–21

Seasonal Color:
Violet

As with God's mercy and grace, so also with God's love—it reveals God as the One who cares for creation. God's mercy gives hope to the weary. God's grace gives new life to all who believe. God's love gives light to the world. In Jesus Christ the fullness of God is made known once and for all. So hope in Christ that you may be strong; have faith and receive the gift that is eternal; live in love and let the light shine. "For God so loved the world . . ."

Call to Worship
LEADER: By grace you have been saved through faith; and this is not your own doing, it is the gift of God.

RESPONSE: For we are God's handiwork, created in Christ Jesus for good works, which God prepared beforehand, that we should walk in them.

(Author's adaptation)

LEADER: Let us worship God.

Prayer of Praise and Adoration
God of infinite goodness and mercy, we cannot escape your presence. Your promise remains with us in every situation. When we are desolate, your Spirit comes to comfort us. Amid our tribulation, your Chosen One remains our firm hope. We can sing your song in whatever land we find our abode. We shall forever give thanks for the gift of your grace. You are God, who never forsakes us. To you be praise and glory.

Prayer of Confession
UNISON: O God, in Christ Jesus you proclaimed your love for all creation. Have mercy on us as we confess our sin. We have overpopulated the earth and violated its goodness. We have depleted nature of its vital resources. Pollution besets us, waters lie stagnant. We care not for ourselves as temples, nor for communities as buildings not built with hands. We plead for forgiveness and ask for your guidance. Help us to be disciplined in taking care of your gifts, lest in neglecting them we lose them forever.

Assurance of Pardon

LEADER: Know that God is rich in mercy. Even though we are dead through our trespasses, God's great love for us makes us alive through Jesus the Christ. We are thus saved by God's grace. Live in the assurance that, as we confess our sin, through Christ's intercession on our behalf we are forgiven.

Prayer of Dedication

O God of boundless love, you restore our strength through faith in your goodness. You look with favor upon us and through Christ redeem us. You take not yourself from us, but promise your presence through the gift of your Spirit. You come from behind to push us, and go before us as our guide. Accept now what we bring you in response to your encompassing care of us.

Prayer of Thanksgiving and Intercession

O God of light and life, through the ages your messengers have proclaimed that your day is at hand. Creation has spoken of your care and benevolent love. You sent the Christ into the midst of humanity, so that there could be no denying your concern for our well-being. You are God, who restores that which your people destroy; you mend brokenness and bring wholeness in the midst of fractured relations. You make wars to cease, and establish peace among all nations. We hear your word for our time, and give thanks for your unending pursuit of righteousness. Send forth your light so that all may inherit your eternal life.

Reform those who disregard how creation depends on your grace. Give them a sense of how all things ought to cohere. You have instilled in us such awesome power; grant us humility to acknowledge your gift and exercise it humanely. Make us aware of how fragile life is, that any one part cannot be abused without affecting the whole. Help us work toward a rightly ordered creation, whatever our role or status.

We pray for those whose relationships are in disarray. Keep us from premature or harmful judgments that only enhance the pain. Help us to offer reconciling suggestions when they can be helpful, and make our presence beneficial in overcoming the incipient loneliness. You have taught us what it means to love one another. You have shown how interdependent all creation ought to be. Keep us mindful of the mutual support we can offer one another, and make us willing to bear another's burden as though it were our own. Let us thereby shed some light on what it means to love others, as you so love the world.

FIFTH SUNDAY IN LENT

Lectionary Readings for the Day
Ps. 51:10–17; Jer. 31:31–34

Heb. 5:7–10; John 12:20–33

Seasonal Color:
Violet

The old passes away, the new emerges. The grain of wheat falls to the earth and dies. From it springs the stalk that in time produces much fruit. Death's sting is tempered by the promise of new life. Do not cling to old ways that hinder your ability to realize the hope of the gospel. Rather, let what you glean from the past lead to fresh insight, so that you may mature in faith.

Call to Worship
LEADER: O God, open thou my lips.

RESPONSE: And my mouth shall show forth thy praise.

LEADER: Create in me a clean heart, O God, and put a new and right spirit within me.

RESPONSE: Restore to me the joy of thy salvation, and uphold me with a willing spirit.

Prayer of Praise and Adoration
O God, who fashioned the covenant and sealed it with the promise of life everlasting, we praise you for mercies that are boundless and sure. Your ways are just, your grace is unending. Fill us now with your Spirit, as we gather before you; and teach us your way, for we seek to be faithful.

Prayer of Confession
UNISON: O God of forgiveness, we pray for new life as we confess our old ways. We hear of your promise amid our own sense of self-doubt. Hope is proclaimed, yet we seek guarantees. Christ calls us to obedience, but we set conditions. When called on to follow, we ask to what end. We applaud commitment, but we treasure our comfort. Forgive our reluctance to walk in newness of life.

Assurance of Pardon
LEADER: Although he was as we are, Jesus "learned obedience through what he suffered; and being made perfect he became the source of eternal salvation to all who obey him." Today, as we come before God confessing our sins, Jesus the high priest is our source of forgiveness. Trust in the word of Christ and be forgiven.

Prayer of Dedication

Most giving and forgiving God, you provide for our every need. You open our lips to offer you praise. You strengthen our hands to respond to Christ's call. With hearts, hands, and voices renewed by your Spirit, we place now before you our commitment to serve. Use us in ways that will benefit others, and accept what we offer as a sign of our faith.

Prayer of Praise and Supplication

Great God of the universe, you open our lips to give you praise. We thank you for the psalmist of old who sings of deliverance. The words lift our spirits as we hear of your faithfulness. We praise you for the prophets who foresaw your promise. They teach us to obey you with total allegiance. We praise you for Christ Jesus, our source of salvation. Through him we are able to approach you in prayer. We praise you for the Holy Spirit, who gives a glimpse of your glory. We receive counsel and guidance to go forth and serve.

Deliver us from all that prevents us from singing your song: from bitterness toward others who hurt or take advantage of us, from fear and insecurity when the future confronts us with a sense of the unknown, from thinking of ourselves so highly that we fail to notice those who need us, from failure to speak out on behalf of those whom society no longer heeds, and from despair when our acts amount to very little when the needs are so great.

As Jeremiah proclaimed allegiance written on the hearts of humanity, let us be diligent in discerning the hope of your salvation. Turn bitterness into understanding, and make us willing to care about even those who would hurt us. Replace our fear with the assurance that you know of our needs; help us to find comfort in Jesus, who endured the cross for us. Give us humble hearts, so that we hear the cries of our neighbors, and give us soothing voices to speak comforting words to them.

We seek to please you, O God of all glory. What we offer, you have implanted within us. What springs forth from our efforts, you have nourished and allowed to blossom. All praise be unto you for that Seed of salvation, Christ Jesus, who puts the song of new life on our lips.

PASSION SUNDAY/PALM SUNDAY

Lectionary Readings for the Day
Ps. 118:19–29; Isa. 50:4–9a
Phil. 2:5–11; Mark 11:1–11

Seasonal Color:
Red

Jesus prepares to enter Jerusalem. He will enter majestically, hearing cries of "Hosanna in the highest!" His sights are set on what he must do; his intentions are faithful to God, who sustains him. Soon the crowds will disperse, to be replaced by tormentors; adulation will cease, and he will be faced with betrayal. Humiliation and obedience lead to death so that life may abound to God's glory.

Call to Worship
LEADER: This is the day which God has made.
RESPONSE: Let us rejoice and be glad in it.
LEADER: Blessed are those who enter in God's name.
RESPONSE: We bless you from the house of the Sovereign One!
LEADER: O give thanks to God, for God is good.
RESPONSE: God's steadfast love endures for ever!

(Author's adaptation)

Prayer of Praise and Adoration
We praise you, O God, for your faithfulness through the ages. You are with us as we greet the dawn of a new day. Your word guides us as we seek to be obedient. You comfort us during times of distress, and judge us according to your righteousness. As you sent Jesus to fulfill your promise, now fill us with your Spirit and bless our worship in Christ's name.

Prayer of Confession
UNISON: Eternal God of mercy, hear us as we confess our sin. Daily we awaken to the new life you give us, yet we fail to be thankful for the rest we have received. Moments await our decision to serve you, yet time passes away as we think only of ourselves. Our routine affords us the chance to minister to others, yet we are absorbed with our own self-improvement. The day is soon passed; it has been much the same as the others. Forgive us for casting aside the precious time you have given.

Assurance of Pardon
LEADER: Hear these words of assurance: Even though Jesus was in the form of God, he "did not count equality with God a thing

to be grasped." Rather, "he humbled himself and became obedient unto death, even unto death on a cross." He died for us, so that we might have life and approach God's throne of judgment cleansed of our sin. In Christ we are forgiven.

Prayer of Dedication

O God of wisdom, you open our eyes to behold the wonder of your mighty acts. You free our tongues to proclaim as good news Christ's suffering for us all. We sing, "Hosanna in the highest!" Christ has entered our lives. Accept now these offerings as our garlands of welcome, and hear our shouts of praise as we seek to follow him.

Prayer of Thanksgiving and Supplication

O God of the prophets and the psalmist, of Mark and of Paul, we thank you for their testimony to your abiding presence. Through times of trial you accompany your people. For those who seek wisdom, you enlighten the mind. You loosen the tongue of the one who stammers, and open the eyes of those whose vision is dimmed. Amid the clamor of noisy parades, you are in the excitement and laughter. When the gathering disperses and your people are lonely, your voice quiets their fears.

Be with us now when we face our trials. Let them not be so overpowering that we succumb to their force. Give us the strength to withstand the pressure, and courage to face boldly those times when our faith is tested. Confronted by those seeking our counsel, we implore your word to illumine our guidance. Help us to offer appropriate options, and to assist our sisters and brothers to choose wisely as they make decisions.

Let us not be reserved in proclaiming Christ's gospel. Keep us free from the fear of embarrassing ourselves. Give us the joy that makes constraint inappropriate, the assurance of new life that makes us willing to take risks. Set us in the midst of those who are seeking salvation. Help us to stand with them long enough to trust us, so together we can learn how Christ sets people free.

Give us patience to sit with the lonely, those for whom crowds pose an unpleasant threat. If they seek comfort, open our arms to embrace them. If they need assurance, free our tongues from stammering, so we can offer them words of confidence. If their sense of well-being is plagued by unseen foes or forces, let our words of witness rehearse how Christ disarms the demons. Through times of trial, you do indeed accompany your people. We sense your Spirit moving among us as we go forth to serve others in Christ's name.

all the ends of the

earth shall remember

THE RESURRECTION OF THE LORD
EASTER DAY

Lectionary Readings for the Day
Ps. 118:14–24; Isa. 25:6–9
I Cor. 15:1–11; Mark 16:1–8

Seasonal Color:
White

The women bring spices to anoint the body of their slain leader. Instead, they are told "He has risen" and gone on to Galilee as foretold. God has rolled back the stone, the covering cast over all peoples, the veil spread over all nations. Death is swallowed up forever. Henceforth there shall be gladness and rejoicing; Christ reigns eternally, so that all may have life.

Call to Worship
LEADER: Christ is risen!
RESPONSE: Christ is risen indeed!
LEADER: This is the day which God has made.
RESPONSE: Let us rejoice and be glad in it.

Prayer of Praise and Adoration
O God, who was, is, and evermore shall be, to you belong all praise and glory. Angels in heaven announce the dawn of your eternal order; trumpets herald Christ's victory as the stone is rolled away; our mouths are opened to proclaim your mercies. We lift up our hearts to you, our Judge and Redeemer.

Litany of Affirmation
LEADER: Truly I perceive that God shows no partiality, but in every nation any one who fears God and does what is right is acceptable to God.
RESPONSE: By the grace of God I am what I am.
LEADER: God raised Jesus on the third day and made him manifest to those God chose, who ate and drank with him after he rose from the dead.
RESPONSE: By the grace of God I am what I am.
LEADER: God commanded us to preach to the people, and to testify that Christ is the one ordained by God to be judge of the living and the dead.
RESPONSE: By the grace of God I am what I am.
LEADER: To him all the prophets bear witness that every one who believes in him receives forgiveness of sins through his name.*

*Acts 10:34, 40, 42, 43; author's adaptation.

RESPONSE: By the grace of God I am what I am, and his grace toward me was not in vain.

Prayer of Dedication

O God, giver of life, who sends the dawn and fills us with hope, we come now before you, bringing our gifts. We cannot repay you for your undying mercy; our gestures are feeble compared to your love. As we commit our days to proclaiming Christ's gospel, accept these offerings as a pledge of our faith. Today is the first day of the rest of our lives.

Prayer of Thanksgiving

Most merciful God, we come before you with all praise and honor, giving thanks for your faithfulness in raising Christ Jesus from the dead. You have set our feet upon the sacred ground of your holy mountain and flung wide the doors of your holy temple. The curtain is rent and we behold your glory, the glory of your only begotten Son, who now intercedes for us.

We give you thanks that because he lived, died, and rose again we have gained a vision of your eternal order. Because he stooped to minister to the least of your people, we too have hope that can lift our spirits out of despair. Since he taught us how to love our neighbor, dividing walls of hostility may no longer keep us apart. When the angels proclaimed his coming to bring peace among nations, we gained a glimpse of your promise that swords shall be beaten into plowshares.

We give you thanks that through Christ your law is written indelibly within us. No longer can we claim that you hide yourself from us. As we seek to serve others, your Holy Spirit is with us. When we face troubled times, you are the source of our comfort and strength. Christ calls us and teaches us what it means to follow your will for us; in our search for maturity, your wisdom prevails.

We give you thanks that all our days can now be lived with assurance, with confidence that in Christ we may dwell in your favor. Remove all hesitation as we step out to greet the dawn of your endless Easter. Fill us with hope as we behold Christ's resurrection. Let us view from your mountain how deserts spring forth with blossoms, how valleys are uplifted and high places made low. We enter your temple to dine with our risen Savior, to break the bread that sustains us and to drink the cup of new life.

SECOND SUNDAY OF EASTER

Lectionary Readings for the Day

Ps. 133

Acts 4:32–35; I John 1:1 to 2:2; John 20:19–31

Seasonal Color:
White

Jesus appears and offers peace to the disciples. He shows them his hands and his side, sends them forth into the world, and gives them the gift of the Holy Spirit. With God's grace to guide them, they witness to Christ's resurrection, sharing their gifts with those who are in need. The truth of God's love has brought light to the world. Let all who have seen that light strive to live in it, so that Christ's promise of peace may dispel the darkness of need.

Call to Worship

LEADER: This is the message we have heard and proclaim to you, that God is light and in God is no darkness at all.

RESPONSE: Behold, how good it is when sisters and brothers live together in unity!

(Author's adaptation)

LEADER: Let us worship God, expressing our unity and praising God's name for bringing light to the world.

Prayer of Praise and Adoration

O God, you bring the dawn of each new day; we praise your name for sending Christ with the promise of new life. You scatter the clouds of darkness so that our eyes can behold the truth of your love. You replace the finality of death with an affirmation of life without ending. We await fresh signs of your loving care as we worship in Christ's name.

Litany of Affirmation and Assurance

LEADER: That which was from the beginning, which we have heard and seen with our eyes concerning the word of life, we proclaim to you.

RESPONSE: God of light, in whom is no darkness, we praise you.

LEADER: The life was made manifest, and we testify to it.

RESPONSE: God of light, in whom is no darkness, we praise you.

LEADER: If we say we have fellowship with God while we walk in darkness, we lie and do not live according to the truth.

RESPONSE: God of light, in whom is no darkness, we praise you.

LEADER: If we confess our sins, Jesus Christ is faithful and just, and will forgive our sins and cleanse us from all unrighteousness.

RESPONSE: Jesus Christ is the expiation for our sins, and not for ours only but also for the sins of the whole world.

(Author's adaptation)

Prayer of Dedication

Source of life, who raised Christ from the dead, all that we have reflects your eternal love. As those in the infant church in Jerusalem brought gifts for those in need, so we too bring offerings as a sign of our commitment and concern. Accept them as our testimony to Christ's resurrection, and cause them to be distributed so that others may live.

Prayer of Thanksgiving and Supplication

Loving God, you dry the tears of those who weep and bring hope and comfort to all who mourn; we give you thanks for the peace of Christ and the signs of his sovereignty over life. We cannot hide from your presence, O Holy One; our needs are all known to you. We are an open book to the One who created us. You have sent Jesus to be our intercessor and redeemer. We give you thanks that through him we can approach you with trust and confidence.

We give thanks for your providence and care for creation. You reign supreme in spite of suspicion, destruction, and greed. Implant within us the peace that Christ bestowed upon his frightened disciples. Send us forth in the Spirit, with wisdom to resolve differences, grace to pray for those who hate us, and vision to strive for harmony in the midst of discord and strife.

We give thanks for the forgiveness offered freely to all through Christ's resurrection from the dead. From now on we can live confident of your grace. Help us to awaken to the assurance of Easter, and to be more attuned to the mercy you bestow. Deliver us from bondage to limits both real and imagined, from principalities and powers that seek to crush us. Let the light of Christ dispel the shadows, making bright the pathway you would have us walk. You are the source of our sanctuary, the haven to whom we turn in times of distress. You are the judge of our decisions and actions. We give you thanks for your abiding forbearance as promised in Christ.

Lectionary Readings for the Day

Ps. 4

Acts 3:12–19; I John 3:1–7; Luke 24:35–48

Seasonal Color:
White

Jesus proclaims the fulfillment of God's covenant, and the disciples are helped to understand the words of Scripture. The lame walk, sins are forgiven, the hungry are fed, the promise of wholeness abides in Christ's purifying atonement. Henceforth, those who believe will be clothed with power to perform acts of compassion and mercy, ministering to others in the name of Christ, who died that all may live!

Call to Worship

LEADER: O God, be gracious to me and hear my prayer.

RESPONSE: Know that God has set us apart and hears us when we call.

LEADER: O God, lift up the light of your countenance upon us.

RESPONSE: O God, be gracious to us and hear our prayer.

(Author's adaptation)

Prayer of Praise and Adoration

Author of life, you have given us breath to praise you, eyes to behold your mercy, and words to proclaim your abiding love. Breathe upon us the promised Holy Spirit, that our minds may be opened to your wisdom and our tongues may boldly declare that you alone are God, through Jesus Christ our Savior.

Litany of Affirmation

LEADER: See what love God has given us, that we should be called God's children.

RESPONSE: What God foretold by the mouths of the prophets, God fulfilled.

LEADER: It does not yet appear what we shall be, but we know that when God appears we shall be in God's likeness.

RESPONSE: What God foretold by the mouths of the prophets, God fulfilled.

LEADER: Every one who thus hopes in God is made pure, as God is pure.

RESPONSE: What God foretold by the mouths of the prophets, God fulfilled.

LEADER: Whoever does right is righteous, as God is righteous.
RESPONSE: What God foretold by the mouths of the prophets, God fulfilled.

(Author's adaptation)

Prayer of Dedication

Giver of eternal gladness, Fountain of life from whom flow endless blessings, all that we have is a gift from you. Accept now these offerings of thanksgiving, symbols of our grateful response to Christ's sacrifice for us. Use our gifts to spread the good news of repentance and forgiveness of sins. May they bring times of refreshment as results of Christ's presence.

Prayer of Thanksgiving and Supplication

O God of Abraham and Sarah, our ancestors in faith, by your grace we have been made, with them, a part of family. You call us your children, and so we are. You watch over our coming and going; you nurture our growth with sustaining wisdom. You send your Spirit as a guide for our wanderings, and give the promise of Christ's redeeming love to rescue us from waywardness.

We thank you for the innocence of children, their trusting natures. Teach us that same love and trust as we look to you for aid. Their dependence leaves them vulnerable to those in whose care they are placed; may they remind us of the obedience of Christ to the One who sent him into the world. Help our children to teach us what it means to be dependent on Another, and give us some measure of their humility as we seek to be faithful.

We thank you for curiosity that leads to learning, for the willingness to move beyond what is already known. Use the spirit of inquiry to prod us out of complacency; make us impatient to know more of your truth. By the gift of your Spirit, give us an insatiable longing to see your will accomplished. Guide us to the Scriptures in search of wisdom, and give us the discipline to pursue the quest.

We thank you for trials that test our allegiance, and the brokenness within that is the prelude to new growth. When we shy away from suffering, confront us with the courage of Jesus, who endured on our behalf. When we avoid sacrifice, chasten us with your judgment and fill us anew with zeal for the reign of God.

You have called us your children and made us members of the household of God. Help us to grow as faithful brothers and sisters in response to your trust.

FOURTH SUNDAY OF EASTER

Lectionary Readings for the Day
Ps. 23
Acts 4:8–12; I John 3:18–24; John 10:11–18

Seasonal Color:
White

The stone rejected by the builders has become the head of the corner. God in Jesus Christ has established the household of believers, who will henceforth be known as the church. As a shepherd cares for the sheep, so also will Christ watch over his followers. As they enter the household, they will be fed, protected, cared for, and led to ventures in faith. A solid foundation and benevolent care are the marks of God's sacrificial love.

Call to Worship
LEADER: [God] is my shepherd; I shall not be in want.
RESPONSE: You spread a table before me in the presence of those who trouble me.
LEADER: You have anointed my head with oil, and my cup is running over.
RESPONSE: Surely your goodness and mercy shall follow me all the days of my life.
UNISON: And I will dwell in the house of [God] forever.

(BCP)

Prayer of Praise and Adoration
All praise be unto you, O God, Great Shepherd of the sheep. You gather your people as lambs to your bosom; you enfold them with your all-embracing love. You refresh us like a stream flowing freely with living waters; you nourish us like a host whose table is heavy-laden. We gather to hear your refreshing word of promise and direction, to honor your name as our guardian and hope.

Litany of Affirmation
LEADER: Little children, let us love not in word or speech but in deed and in truth.
RESPONSE: All who keep God's commandments abide in God, and God abides in them.
LEADER: By this we shall know that we are of the truth, for God knows everything.
RESPONSE: All who keep God's commandments abide in God, and God abides in them.

LEADER: Beloved, if our hearts do not condemn us, we have confidence before God.

RESPONSE: All who keep God's commandments abide in God, and God abides in them.

LEADER: This is what God commands: believe in the name of Christ Jesus and love one another.

RESPONSE: And by this we know that God abides in us, by the Spirit which God has given us.

(Author's adaptation)

Prayer of Dedication

Source of healing, Bringer of wholeness, you enter the world and cause the light to shine, the lame to walk, the sins of all to be forgiven. Whatever we bring you is a gift of your graciousness; all that we offer, you have poured out upon us. Use us and mold us to conform to your will for all people; take our talents and apply them to spread the truth of your love.

Prayer of Thanksgiving and Supplication

God of the universe and all that dwells therein, great is your name. You are worthy of all our praise. You sent Jesus of Nazareth to redeem us from sin. You raised him from the dead, and seated him at your right hand. He knows our inmost thoughts, our fears and rejoicings; he walked this earth as we do, yet without straying from the course you designed. As a shepherd, he watches over us even at this moment.

We pray for all those who wander this day in the wilderness of broken covenants and confused goals. Give them an awareness of your presence amid their faltering steps, and a sense of direction which will lead them to safety. Keep us from judging them as somehow weak or inferior because they appear aimless or lost. Help us to lend them our understanding as they seek to find their way. Remind us of our own wanderings and our constant need for guidance from you.

We pray for all those entrapped by whatever snare restrains them. Loose them and make them free, as Christ was free, to do your will. You sent your Word, Jesus Christ, to show what humanity was intended to be; send now your Spirit to form in us that new creation.

Our Savior promised to search for the stray, give guidance to the aimless, and direct the course of those who are lost. We pray for the Shepherd's encompassing care as we in Christ's name commit ourselves to do likewise.

FIFTH SUNDAY OF EASTER

Lectionary Readings for the Day
Ps. 22:25–31
Acts 8:26–40; I John 4:7–12; John 15:1–8

Seasonal Color:
White

To bear fruit is both a gift and a responsibility. Nourishment flows through the vine, bringing gifts of beauty as leaves and buds appear. Cultivation and care coax the fruit to maturity in time for the harvest. There is both promise and judgment as Christ calls his disciples to go and bear fruit. With the promise of God's sustenance, believers will be judged by the gifts of love they produce.

Call to Worship
LEADER: From thee comes my praise in the great congregation.
RESPONSE: My vows I will pay before those who fear God.
LEADER: All the ends of the earth shall remember and turn to God.
RESPONSE: And all the families of the nations shall worship before God.

Prayer of Praise and Adoration
Ruler of nations, you have dominion over all the earth. We praise your name and bow down before you. You bring pride to the humble, and cause the boastful to be brought low. The afflicted find hope through your mercy; the comfortable you challenge and chasten. As your wisdom led our fathers and mothers throughout the ages, make us receptive to the testimony of your love, for we pray in the name of Christ Jesus, the Word made flesh.

Litany of Affirmation
LEADER: Beloved, let us love one another; for love is of God, and whoever loves is born of God and knows God.
RESPONSE: If we love one another, God abides in us.
LEADER: In this the love of God was made manifest among us, that God sent Jesus Christ into the world.
RESPONSE: If we love one another, God abides in us.
LEADER: In this is love, not that we loved God but that God loved us and sent Jesus to be the expiation for our sins.

RESPONSE: If we love one another, God abides in us.
LEADER: Beloved, if God so loved us, we also ought to love one another.
RESPONSE: If we love one another, God abides in us and God's love is perfected in us.

Prayer of Dedication

Your love, O God, is perfected in us through the gift of your chosen one, Christ Jesus. All that we have reflects a measure of his atoning sacrifice poured out on behalf of us all. Accept what we give to you as we respond to Christ's loving-kindness, and enhance what we do, so that others may experience your tenderness. Cultivate us to bear more fruit to the glory of your name.

Prayer of Thanksgiving and Supplication

Eternal God, we thank you for Jesus, who brought hope to the distressed, promise to the despairing, and healing to the afflicted. In him there is the gift of life eternal to all who believe. We thank you for your Holy Spirit, who calls us to labor. As Christ is the vine, you name us the branches and send us forth to bear much fruit.

Let love lead us to be more forgiving, and add to love the discipline to be a reconciling force in the world. When enemies taunt us, assure us of your presence as we seek patience and inner strength. Amid tensions caused by misunderstanding, suspicion, or lack of trust, send your Spirit of insight and hope. Help us make the first move toward those we have offended, forsaking our pride in seeking peace.

Let love lead us to be more daring; give us the boldness to speak out on behalf of the voiceless. Let us not be afraid to venture into dark places, or into situations in which we are not in control. Fill us with the confidence that you will not desert us, the assurance that what we do is in accord with your will. Keep us from becoming frustrated by the many faces of evil, and set our sights on those injustices that we can overcome.

Let love lead us to be more trusting; give us the faith to make Christ supreme in our lives. Help us translate our words of confession into acts of compassion, our desire to be faithful into deeds of obedience. Your love does indeed work wonders. Work now in us, so that others may behold your love.

SIXTH SUNDAY OF EASTER

Lectionary Readings for the Day
Ps. 98

Acts 10:44–48; I John 5:1–6; John 15:9–17

Seasonal Color:
White

Filled with joy, Jesus' disciples are no longer called servants but friends. Jesus has laid down his life for his followers, so that their life may be complete in his love. As friends of Jesus, they are to go and do as he commands, baptizing others in the name of Jesus Christ and performing acts of love.

Call to Worship
LEADER: Make a joyful noise, all the earth!
RESPONSE: Break forth in joyous song to the God of victory!
LEADER: Let the sea roar, and all that fills it; the world and those who dwell in it!

(Author's adaptation)

RESPONSE: With trumpets and the sound of the horn we make a joyful noise as we worship God.

Prayer of Praise and Adoration
O God of power and majesty, as the sea roars, your name is praised. Waves pounding the shore remind us of your grandeur. By your creative design, birds fly, fish swim, and creatures in forests and meadows leap and run. All creation chants in praise of your plan for them. As you make our joy complete in the gift of your only begotten Son, Christ Jesus our Savior, we worship you with hearts, hands, and voices in songs of glad adoration.

Litany of Affirmation
LEADER: Every one who believes that Jesus is the Christ is a child of God, and every one who loves the parent loves the child.
RESPONSE: For this is the love of God, that we keep God's commandments.
LEADER: By this we know that we love the children of God, when we love God and obey God's commandments.
RESPONSE: For this is the love of God, that we keep God's commandments.
LEADER: For whatever is born of God overcomes the world; and this is the victory that overcomes the world, our faith.

RESPONSE: For this is the love of God, that we keep God's commandments.

LEADER: Who overcomes the world? Those who believe that Jesus is the Christ.

RESPONSE: For this is the love of God, that we keep God's commandments. And God's commandments are not burdensome.

Prayer of Dedication

O God, as the Holy Spirit fell on all who heard your word, so fill us as we come before you in response to Christ's gift of love. By your Spirit, enable us to bear fruit and overcome the world with our faith. Accept our gifts as the first signs of a bountiful harvest, and our commitment to labor on behalf of all your children. Through our work, may they be led to believe in your word.

Prayer of Thanksgiving and Intercession

O God of righteousness and equity, you speak and the earth responds with sounds of thanksgiving; you act and the nations attest to your victory. We thank you for your word that teaches us to trust in you. We thank you for your actions and the promises you fulfill: for Christ Jesus, whose sacrifice restores us to goodness because of your mercy; for the Holy Spirit, whose guidance enables us to seek justice, to love kindness, and to walk humbly with you.

We pray for those who wonder when justice will come to them. They cry out for equity, but their pleas go unheard. As you brought vindication to the Israelites when the hosts rose up against them, bring a sense of your justice to those who are wronged and misused. Give us compassion to stand with them, courage to speak on their behalf, and commitment to work for change in those systems that work against them.

We give thanks for all those who show kindness without thought of their own gain. They are the saints of Christ's household who glide gracefully from chore to chore. Bestow upon them a measure of strength to match their diligence; reward them with a sense of accomplishment equal to their level of patience. Forbid, O God, that we should ever take them for granted.

We pray for all sisters and brothers who seek to walk humbly with you. Help us to support one another in the quest to live simply; guide us to note afresh the many blessings you give us. In all that we do together, hear our shouts of thanksgiving.

SEVENTH SUNDAY OF EASTER

Lectionary Readings for the Day
Ps. 1

Acts 1:15–17, 21–26;

I John 5:9–13; John 17:11b–19

Seasonal Color:
White

Jesus prays for his followers, that they may be kept safe. They are sent into the world armed with God's word and sanctified in the truth. For their sake Christ consecrates himself. The world may hate them, but there is no escape from involvement within it. Henceforth Christ's followers will go into all nations, proclaiming the truth of God's love and radiating the joy of new life. They are given the assurance of God's protection as Christ intercedes on their behalf.

Call to Worship
LEADER: Blessed are those who take delight in God's law.

RESPONSE: They are like trees that yield fruit in season, and whose leaves do not wither.

LEADER: Let us meditate on God's law both by day and by night.

(Author's adaptation)

RESPONSE: May God number us with the righteous as we worship.

Prayer of Praise and Adoration
To meditate upon your law, O God, is to learn of your love and know of your righteousness. You are a God of tender mercy, whose benevolent care protects your children and all creation. We gather to worship you as creatures of righteousness, made whole by the redeeming love of Jesus the Christ. Open our hearts to sing of your goodness, our minds to explore your wisdom, and our lips to give you praise.

Litany of Affirmation
LEADER: The testimony of God is greater than human testimony. God's testimony has borne witness to Jesus, the Christ.

RESPONSE: Whoever receives the Word of God has life.

LEADER: Whoever believes in the One whom God sent has God's testimony.

RESPONSE: Whoever receives the Word of God has life.

LEADER: The testimony is this: God gave us eternal life, and this life is in Jesus Christ, God's Anointed One.

RESPONSE: Whoever receives the Word of God has life.

LEADER: I proclaim this to you who confess the name of Jesus Christ, that you may know that you have eternal life.

RESPONSE: Whoever receives the Word of God has life.

(Author's adaptation)

Prayer of Dedication

Armed with the truth of your love, O Shield and Defender, you send us into the world to radiate the joy of new life. Accept our efforts, and make them productive in fulfilling your will. Enhance our gifts with the empowerment of your Holy Spirit. In all we do, challenge us to be obedient to the call of Jesus Christ, to walk in faithfulness, and to respond to the tasks you assign us.

Prayer of Thanksgiving and Supplication

God of wisdom, power, and majesty, who are we that you should look with favor upon us? Yet you have written your law upon our hearts, that we may know of your righteousness. You have sent the prophets; they teach us obedience. Your Spirit guides us; we have assurance that you will never forsake us. Christ Jesus reveals all that we know of you. We give you thanks for his redeeming love in spite of our wayward behavior. We claim the benefits of his sacrifice on our behalf.

Help us to be still, so that we can hear you speak. Amid the babble of human speech, give us ears to listen to your voice. As demands are made and pressures mount, put us at ease and sustain us by your presence. As we meditate on the love of Jesus, may the hope he gives be a haven of rest and renewal.

Help us to find the discipline to be more faithful. Time passes quickly, and our tasks are undone. Translate our desires into commitment; keep us from putting off decisions that demand energy and effort. Send your Holy Spirit to guide us when the way seems unsure, and instill within us that measure of confidence which will enable us to act.

Enlighten us with your wisdom. Awaken us to the abiding testimony of your covenant; illumine the dark places of our nagging doubts. By your power, make us bolder and better disciples. Give us the courage to forsake the easy life and risk personal security so that others may learn of your love. In your majesty, keep us ever conscious of our dependence on you, and ready to give you praise.

the leaves in the trees

shiver with delight

THE DAY OF PENTECOST

Lectionary Readings for the Day
Ps. 104:24–34; Ezek. 37:1–14

Acts 2:1–21; John 15:26–27; 16:4b–15

Seasonal Color:
Red

The gift of the Holy Spirit brings guidance to humanity, glory to Christ, and clarity of God's righteousness. Henceforth God's people shall be led to behold the extent of God's truth. Christ's name is to be praised in all they do. He intercedes on behalf of their weaknesses, and promises to uphold them when judgment occurs. With the gift of empowerment, all things are now possible, so long as they occur in God's name.

Call to Worship
LEADER: May the glory of God endure for ever, may God rejoice in all God's works.

RESPONSE: I will sing to God as long as I live, I will sing praise to my Redeemer while I have being.

LEADER: May my meditation be pleasing to God, for I rejoice in God.

RESPONSE: Give thanks to God, O my soul! Let all people praise God!

(Author's adaptation)

Prayer of Praise and Adoration
Give thanks to God, O my soul, and all that is within me praise God's holy name. We come, O God, to give you honor and glory. We gather to bless you for your countless gifts. Alive with your Spirit and made whole by Christ's love, we praise your name. The heavens portray the extent of your wisdom; the earth is full of your handiwork. We join in creation's song, lauding your name with the glad praises we bring.

Prayer of Confession
UNISON: O God, like bones in the desert our faith is dried up and lifeless. The winds of false doctrine sear our spirits; the heat of conflict saps our strength. We seek an oasis to escape your judgment; we wander aimlessly in search of direction. Have mercy upon us, and fill us anew with your Spirit. Give us counsel and guidance, and forgive us our waywardness.

Assurance of Pardon

LEADER: The prophet Joel declares that in the last days God's Spirit will be poured out upon all flesh. "And it shall be that whoever calls on God shall be saved." Know that as you call on God's name, Christ intercedes on your behalf to deliver you in his righteousness, blameless before God.

Prayer of Dedication

O God of deliverance, with a right spirit within us we pour out our gifts in your presence. Take us and use us as you see fit. Where speaking can bring a sense of your righteousness, we offer our voices to proclaim your will. Where our efforts can free others from bondage, we offer our strength to help in time of need. We bring ourselves to be used for Christ's sake. Show us the way, and we will respond.

Prayer of Thanksgiving and Supplication

Almighty God, you speak and the heavens tremble; you move and the leaves of the trees shiver with delight. The babble of waters on their course to the sea attests to your wisdom and plan for creation. A child does not cry without your hearing it; as a parent you brood over young ones and watch their coming and going. No one and no thing can evade your watchful presence. We give you thanks that you see fit even to dwell in our midst.

We are amazed by your love for us, and moved that you should send your Son to atone for our sins. We give you thanks that he walked this earthly life, suffered as we do, yet remained steadfastly obedient. Give us a measure of his faithfulness. We are not able; lend us the necessary commitment to be his disciples. Grant that our decisions and actions may be in accord with his will for us. Frustrate us when our involvement departs from his path.

We are in awe of the wisdom you continually give us, how you fill us with the Holy Spirit, who offers counsel and guidance. You share our concerns, accompany us amid the routines of the day, and comfort us during times of great anxiety. When our spirits radiate joy, you rejoice with us. Make us grateful to hear your word of discipline, and ready always to return you thanks. Help us to be mindful of your presence with us, and to reflect your indwelling Spirit in all we do.

Guide now our movements and the course of our actions. May we care for others as you care for us. Bring life to our spirits and a sense of joy to our living. Let our days be full of witness to your overwhelming goodness in Christ.

TRINITY SUNDAY

Lectionary Readings for the Day
Ps. 29; Isa. 6:1–8
Rom. 8:12–17; John 3:1–17

Seasonal Color:
White

Jesus teaches what it means to be born of the Spirit. It means being baptized as a sign of God's grace; it means new life unlimited by the frailties of the flesh; it means that those believing in Christ are no longer condemned. Salvation comes as a gift of God's love. Nicodemus asks Jesus for clarity; what he gets is much more. Jesus invites him to believe that life in the Spirit is eternal life.

Call to Worship
LEADER: Give praise to God, O heavenly beings.
RESPONSE: Give praise to God's glory and strength.
LEADER: Give God the glory due God's name.
RESPONSE: Worship God in holy array.
LEADER: The voice of God is powerful.
RESPONSE: The voice of God is full of majesty.
LEADER: May God give strength to God's people.
RESPONSE: May God bless the people with peace!

(Author's adaptation)

Prayer of Praise and Adoration
Holy, holy, holy God, all the earth is full of your majesty. The lightning flash is a sign of your creative voice; thunder resounds with the magnitude of your power and strength. The rains fall as a reminder of your gentle refreshment; the sun shines in testimony to the warmth of your love. All creation is your temple; none can hide from you. Exposed to your grandeur and led by your Spirit, we give you all praise and honor, God of our lives.

Prayer of Confession
UNISON: Source of redeeming grace and infinite goodness, hear us as in Christ we pray for forgiveness. While you reach out to us in fellowship, we turn from you in shame. We do not do what you command. We proclaim not your love, since we seldom serve others. We confess Christ as Savior, yet obey him indifferently, if at all. Our discipleship suffers, for we heed not your guidance. We are in need of repentance as we confess our sins. Have mercy upon us, and grant us your pardon.

Assurance of Pardon

LEADER: After Isaiah had confessed his uncleanliness, a seraph flew to him, carrying a burning coal from the altar. The seraph touched Isaiah and said, "Behold, this has touched your lips; your guilt is taken away, and your sin forgiven." The sacrifice of Christ at the altar of God's eternal grace has touched our lives, and we too can rest in the assurance of God's pardon.

Prayer of Dedication

You beckon us to follow you, O Christ, and to proclaim your salvation to all people everywhere. We are like Isaiah, hearing God's voice and responding, "Here am I! Send me." We offer ourselves at the threshold of your sanctuary, to be sent forth in ministry as the Holy Spirit will guide us.

Prayer of Thanksgiving

O God of revelation, who chose not to remain apart from your people but sent Jesus into the world to enlighten us, we give thanks that in Christ we can know you, and through him find favor as we worship you in thought, word, and deed. By Christ we are taught what it means to obey you: He remained faithful in spite of persecution at the hands of his enemies; he sacrificed his own life, so that those who believe in him might inherit your promise of life everlasting. Give us such courage and conviction, so that in his name we can act with compassion.

In Scripture we are led by the witness of those who have sought to be faithful. We give you thanks for their testimony to the truth of your presence: You spoke through the scribes as they recorded the commandments; you filled the poets with inspiration as they penned their songs of praise and thanksgiving; you gave the prophets dreams of your eternal salvation and visions of your awesome judgment as they called the chosen people to account for their actions. We stand in succession with men and women of all generations: prophets and priests, disciples and teachers, parents and guardians, who testify to your truth.

Through the Holy Spirit, we are convinced that you will eternally guide us along your path of righteousness. The goodly heritage awaits us, thanks to your abiding encouragement. As our hearts are warmed by you, our arms will embrace strangers. As you guide our thinking, our mouths will proclaim your love. As you redeem us from futility, our whole being will be cleansed of impurity. We give thanks for your revelation, which frees us to serve.

SECOND SUNDAY AFTER PENTECOST

Lectionary Readings for the Day
Ps. 20: I Sam. 16:1–13
II Cor. 4:5–12; Mark 2:23 to 3:6

Seasonal Color:
Green

Jesus upsets the authorities with his unorthodox behavior. When the disciples pluck grain on the Sabbath, Jesus reminds the authorities that David ate the bread of the Presence. When Jesus himself heals the man with the withered hand, he asks them if it is harmful to do good on the Sabbath. Do not clutter the day with binding regulations that inhibit the possibility of giving God praise.

Call to Worship
LEADER: What we preach is not ourselves, but Jesus Christ, our redeemer.
RESPONSE: It is the God who said, "Let light shine out of darkness," who has shone in our hearts.
LEADER: Let us in Christ give God the glory. Let us worship God.

Prayer of Praise and Adoration
God our protector and comforter, our shield and defender, hear our glad praises as we boast of your goodness. We gather as witnesses to your redeeming graciousness; we worship in response to your encompassing love. The birds start to sing before the sun even rises, proof that you promise the dawn of new life while it is yet dark. Let your light now shine on our darkness, that we may discern your will for us, giving you the honor due your glorious name.

Prayer of Confession
UNISON: O God, hear our confession, for we still dwell in darkness. We are afflicted and crushed by a sense of inadequacy. When perplexed, we despair that there may be no hope. Persecution leaves us feeling forsaken. When foes strike us down, we assume we're destroyed. We hear that Christ resides like a treasure within us. Transform our whole being so that we live in that truth.

Assurance of Pardon
LEADER: Do not lose heart! God is merciful and just and forgives us our sins. Renounce disgraceful, underhanded ways. Refuse to

practice cunning or to tamper with God's word. Be open to the truth of God's graciousness. In Jesus Christ, we are forgiven.

Prayer of Dedication

O God, you anoint us with the oil of your blessing; you set us apart as Christ calls us to serve. You fill us with the Spirit of righteousness. We are vessels of your holiness, prepared to do what you command. Be pleased with our sacrifices, and take delight in our victories; enhance all our efforts, and multiply their effectiveness. Help us rise to the level of your trust in us, as we dedicate our gifts in response to your goodness.

Prayer of Thanksgiving and Supplication

Creator God, who set aside one day a week as holy, a day of rest for our re-creation, we give you thanks for the liberating message of Jesus, which affirms the day and keeps us from becoming enslaved by it. Save us when we tend to bind ourselves with countless regulations; may Christ speak to us too with authority, and set us free to praise you at all times and in all ways.

Help us to model all our days on this one you call holy. As the disciples plucked heads of grain, give us the bread we need to sustain ourselves. Keep us from wanton craving after an ever-increasing list of goods, things that weigh us down and in time demand so much attention. Help us to be satisfied with the simple necessities of life, and enable us to share our abundance.

As Jesus healed the man with a withered hand, cleanse us from the sin that limits our ability to do good. Remove the scales from our eyes that allow us to see only our own needs. Open our ears, so that we hear Christ's commandment to forsake all and follow him. May our hearts beat with joy at the thought of self-giving service. Give us the good sense to use our time wisely.

As the Pharisees held counsel on how to destroy Jesus, so there are those today who would prefer to have us out of the way. Nevertheless, make us the goads who call others to righteousness, the alarms that sound when the rights of others are disregarded. Help us to ferret out injustice; make us quick to praise goodness whenever it occurs. On this holy day, re-create in us a sense of urgency to be about your business.

THIRD SUNDAY AFTER PENTECOST

Lectionary Readings for the Day
Ps. 57; I Sam. 16:14–23
II Cor. 4:13 to 5:1; Mark 3:20–35

Seasonal Color:
Green

A covenant community is a gathering of individuals with a common experience of being called by God and given a purpose. It is characterized by a common loyalty to God and a shared sense of purpose in the world. In the covenant community, the members are related to one another as organs of the body. When one suffers, all are in pain. The body functions best when all members are present and functioning.

Call to Worship
LEADER: My heart is steadfast, O God, my heart is steadfast! I will sing and make melody!
RESPONSE: I will give thanks to thee, O God, among the peoples; I will sing praises to thee among the nations.
LEADER: For thy steadfast love is great to the heavens, thy faithfulness to the clouds.
RESPONSE: Be exalted, O God, above the heavens! Let thy glory be over all the earth!

Prayer of Praise and Adoration
Our souls awake, O God, to the thrill of your splendor; with our voices we praise you from dawn unto dusk. We greet the new day warmed by your love for us; we rest secure in the night, comforted by the light of your Spirit. Each hour you give us is a moment of blessing, a time to rejoice and abound with new life. "Be exalted, O God, above the heavens! Let thy glory be over all the earth!"

Litany of Affirmation
LEADER: Since we have the same spirit of faith as he had who wrote, "I believed, and so I spoke," we too believe, and so we speak.
RESPONSE: So we do not lose heart. Our inner nature is being renewed every day.
LEADER: Knowing that God who raised the Lord Jesus will raise us also with Jesus and bring us with you into God's presence.
RESPONSE: So we do not lose heart. Our inner nature is being renewed every day.

LEADER: For it is all for your sake, so that as grace extends to more and more people it may increase thanksgiving, to the glory of God.

RESPONSE: So we do not lose heart. Our inner nature is being renewed every day.

Prayer of Dedication

You call forth eternal hope within us, O God; our faith abounds, because of your redeeming grace. With hearts uplifted by the truth of your mercy, and spirits cleansed with the fullness of your indwelling blessing, we come before you, ready and eager to serve. Continue to fashion us until we conform to your will for us; equip us and through Christ make us useful as agents of your all-embracing love.

Prayer of Thanksgiving

Tender and loving God, you bear our afflictions as though they were your own; we give you thanks for our refuge in Jesus, our haven and shelter. In him we see your care for us when we are attacked or aggrieved. In him we see your anger with forces that hinder our obedience. In him we see your compassion for our weakness, and your clear call to rise above our doubts and misgivings. In him we see your firm resolution that nothing shall ultimately separate us from your promised salvation.

We give you thanks for ~~David, and~~ all those whose music dispels gloom and makes hearts lighter. Their harmony brings resolution and accord amid the dissonant sounds of competing forces vying for our attention. Their discipline reminds us of our own need to attune ourselves to your will through obedience and skillful practice. Their melody teaches us to blend our talents with those about us, composing a unison refrain in which all can join. Their gaiety keeps us from taking ourselves and our efforts too seriously, since it is ultimately to you that we sing our praises.

We give you thanks for sisters and brothers, mothers and fathers, and all those who are family to us in the venture of faith. Upon them we rely for nurture and sustenance, support and guidance, and understanding and forgiveness as we search for your truth. We give thanks that we can trust them when all else around us is threatening, and rely on them without feeling ashamed. The household of faith abounds with signs of your tenderness and mercy. We give thanks for Jesus who is the cornerstone, for ~~David~~ who ~~taught~~ us to sing, and for each other, upon whom we rely to show us your love.

FOURTH SUNDAY AFTER PENTECOST

Lectionary Readings for the Day
Ps. 46; II Sam. 1:1, 17–27   *Seasonal Color:*
II Cor. 5:6–10, 14–17; Mark 4:26–34   *Green*

The mystery of the Kingdom of God is like a seed planted. It grows, and we know not how. Sometimes it is helped by our efforts. At other times it is hindered by what we do. It is best for us to remember that it is always God's Kingdom and we are its agents. Let what we do be to God's glory, so that the Kingdom may spread and all may taste the fruits of the harvest.

Call to Worship
LEADER: God is our refuge and strength, a very present help in trouble.
RESPONSE: Therefore we will not fear though the earth should change, though the mountains shake in the heart of the sea.
LEADER: Be still, and know that I am God. I am exalted among the nations, I am exalted in the earth!
RESPONSE: The God of hosts is with us; the God of Jacob is our refuge.

Prayer of Praise and Adoration
God of our refuge, what have we to fear? You are a very present help in times of trouble, a source of comfort during distress. There is no matter so small that you are not aware of it, no problem too great that we cannot share it with you. You who move mountains and set streams on their courses, within your providence you take care even of us. We praise you and honor you, God of creation; you are indeed our refuge and strength.

Litany of Affirmation
LEADER: So we are always of good courage.
RESPONSE: For we walk by faith, not by sight.
LEADER: We know that while we are at home in the body we are away from the risen Christ.
RESPONSE: For we walk by faith, not by sight.
LEADER: We are of good courage, and we would rather be away from the body and at home with the risen Christ.
RESPONSE: For we walk by faith, not by sight.

LEADER: So whether we are at home or away, we make it our aim to please him.
RESPONSE: For we walk by faith, not by sight.
LEADER: For we must all appear before the judgment seat of Christ, so that each one may receive good or evil.
RESPONSE: Let us then continue to walk by faith, not by sight.

Prayer of Dedication

O God, your goodness surrounds us, your grace sustains us, your mercy redeems us; by your love we are saved. We come before you, offering our praise for your indwelling Spirit and giving you thanks for Christ Jesus, who sends us new life. Placing before you the fruits of our labors, we confess anew our trust in your goodness. We rely on your grace; we are in the hands of your mercy as we seek to love others as you command.

Prayer of Thanksgiving and Petition

O God, our refuge and strength, we give you thanks that when we appear before the judgment seat of Christ we can have courage; he intercedes on our behalf. His Spirit chides us out of complacency and goads us away from unfaithful behavior. In spite of our rebellion and betrayal, we can in repentance put ourselves at your mercy.

We give thanks for your covenant, which spans generations. Through Scripture we hear again the promise that you will not forsake us. Those who have gone before now dwell with assurance of your eternal presence. We trust that those who come after us will inherit your favor. We stand in succession of those called your people, redeemed and forgiven, thanks to your grace.

Through Christ's intercession, we are encouraged to pray for your wisdom and guidance. Help us to learn from the struggles of history that weapons are no substitute for feeding the hungry. Make us as eager to help others shape their own destiny as we are zealous in protecting our rights. We need to hear again how to beat swords into plowshares, and spears into pruning hooks, for the mighty keep falling, and threats of war do not cease.

Make us agents of your peace. When we stand before the judgment seat, grant that we shall have acted to ease pain, given refuge to those who needed shelter, and helped the oppressed live with dignity. Through our faithful response, may the naked have been clothed, the sick have been made well. Your encouragement makes us bold. Christ's intercession gives us hope. O Refuge and our Strength, we give you thanks.

FIFTH SUNDAY AFTER PENTECOST

Lectionary Readings for the Day
Ps. 48; II Sam. 5:1–12 *Seasonal Color:*
II Cor. 5:18 to 6:2; Mark 4:35–41 *Green*

There is calmness that comes with faith. When the winds blow and waves threaten the ship of life, we trust in One who will tend our needs. Such care awed the disciples, as Jesus rebuked the wind and ordered the sea to be still. So we too may turn to Jesus in the midst of the perils of life and hear his "Peace! Be still!"

Call to Worship
LEADER: We have thought on thy steadfast love, O God, in the midst of thy temple.
RESPONSE: As thy name, O God, so thy praise reaches to the ends of the earth.
LEADER: Let us worship God.

Prayer of Praise and Adoration
You are great, O God, and deserving of praise. Your works attest to your grandeur; your love exceeds comprehension. Wherever we look, we see signs of your splendor; the good that we do is a result of your grace. You fill your sanctuary with the presence of your Holy Spirit; you send your Word, Jesus, to dwell in our midst. We are surrounded by testimony to your loving goodness; we bow down before you and give you our praise.

Litany of Affirmation
LEADER: All this is from God, who through Christ reconciled us to God and gave us the ministry of reconciliation.
RESPONSE: So we are ambassadors for Christ.
LEADER: In Christ, God was reconciling the world to God, not counting their trespasses against them, and entrusting to us the message of reconciliation.
RESPONSE: So we are ambassadors for Christ.
LEADER: We beseech you on behalf of Christ, be reconciled to God.
RESPONSE: Behold, now is the acceptable time.
LEADER: For our sake God made him to be sin who knew no sin, so that in him we might become the righteousness of God.
RESPONSE: Behold, now is the acceptable time.

Prayer of Dedication

O God, as Christ calls us, your Spirit empowers us. We accept your charge to be his ambassadors for peace. Reconciled by Christ to your loving judgment, we will seek to work righteousness through acts of goodwill. Accept our efforts when they please you, and frustrate our attempts when they do not serve you. Lead us in Christ to become worthy disciples, as, filled with your Spirit, we respond to his call.

Prayer of Thanksgiving and Supplication

O God, if you build the house, who can destroy it? If you establish a covenant, who can defeat your purpose? If you turn against your people in righteous judgment, who can withstand your anger? Yet you have assembled a people and called them your own. You have built mighty temples for your people and accepted their praise. You have set your sign in the heavens that you will never withdraw your blessing, and you have sent Christ as the eternal seal of your love. Nothing can separate us from your redeeming graciousness.

We thank you that you call and name us Christ's church. Make us worthy servants in his name. Set us apart, so that we can witness to your commandment, your reconciliation, your righteousness, and your peace. Help us to build a society where justice reigns, where the weak are empowered, not exploited. Give us a sense of what is right, so that what we do is in accord with Christ's will.

Still within us those turbulent fears of our own making, and those inflicted upon us. When thoughts of inadequacy grip us, remind us of Christ, who hung on the cross that we might live. When we are attacked in pursuit of your righteousness, surround us with the armor of your impenetrable Spirit. When all around us there is evidence of suffering, and when cries of injustice arise from those seeking a sign of compassion, keep us attuned to your call to be ambassadors for Christ and ministers of reconciliation.

Lectionary Readings for the Day
Ps. 24; II Sam. 6:1–15
II Cor. 8:7–15; Mark 5:21–43

Seasonal Color:
Green

Faith makes a woman whole. Faith raises a father's daughter who all feared was dead. Believing in Jesus, the woman touches his garment as he passes. She feels a healing power within her, and she is well again. The child's father too believes in Jesus' miraculous power and intercedes for her. Jesus goes to the little girl and touches her, and she regains consciousness. Faith involves reaching out for help. It also involves hope despite impossible situations. Jesus taught how to reach out and hope in God.

Call to Worship
LEADER: The earth is God's and the fulness thereof, the world and those who dwell therein.
RESPONSE: Lift up your heads, O gates! and be lifted up, O ancient doors! that the God of glory may come in.
LEADER: Let us worship God.

Prayer of Praise and Adoration
O God of all creation, the earth is yours, and the fullness thereof. You touch the leaves with the dew of the morning; you send the breezes to cool the night. The trees are laden with fruit because of your blessing; fields produce crops because of your care. As you watch over your people and fill all their needs, so now send forth your Spirit and be present among us. We lift up our heads and give you praise in Christ's name.

Prayer of Confession
UNISON: God of forgiveness, grant us your favor as we make our confession. You call us to excellence; we fall short of your confidence in us. You grant to us grace; we abuse your gift. You expect our decisions to match your desires, our love to be genuine in obeying your will. Yet we trust our appetites rather than rely on your goodness; we look to our comfort rather than to our neighbor's need. In Christ, have mercy on us and forgive us our sin.

Assurance of Pardon
LEADER: Paul assures us of God's reconciling graciousness when he writes, "You know the grace of our Savior Jesus Christ, that

though he was rich, yet for your sake he became poor, so that by his poverty you might become rich." In Christ we may dwell in the richness of God's favor, and rest assured in the fullness of God's redeeming forgiveness.

Prayer of Dedication
O God, as David brought up the Ark of the Covenant with much dancing and singing, we also rejoice as we offer our gifts. As the Ark held the commandments, may our gifts receive your approval. As the Ark was a sign of your covenant, let our gifts bear witness to your love. As the Ark brought hope to the people, use our gifts to bring relief to the needy. Accept these offerings in response to your graciousness, and may all who receive them find joy in new life.

Prayer of Thanksgiving
O God of the covenant, we give you thanks that Christ has lifted the gates to eternity through his death and resurrection. Your Holy Spirit opens the doors of the sanctuary, wherein we may dwell with assurance of new life. Even as David treasured the Ark of God, the symbol of your presence, and carried it to Jerusalem, so we treasure your word in Scripture and give you thanks for its guidance.

As we hear how your promise led the people to rejoice, and learn of the richness Christ's sacrifice bestowed, we give thanks for the Scriptures which continue to guide us. Their words meet our needs as we heed what they say. We confess that we are not diligent in seeking their direction. Our own desires conflict with what we read therein. Yet we are heartened as we learn afresh of your forgiveness, and trust Christ to lead us as we repent.

We give thanks for the Holy Spirit, who continues to touch us with your everlasting presence. Allow us to experience the healing power of Christ's seamless garment as we face daily the trials that test our faith. We are consoled by the abiding witness of those whose courage continues to uphold them in spite of their suffering. We are led to have hope ourselves, as we give thanks for their trust.

We praise you that not even death itself can erase your promise of life eternal. The memories of those departed attest to the truth that Christ has indeed opened the portals to your heavenly reaches. We hold our heads high and with our voices sing your blessings. Your covenant never ceases, and for that we give you thanks.

SEVENTH SUNDAY AFTER PENTECOST

Lectionary Readings for the Day
Ps. 89:20–37; II Sam. 7:1–17
II Cor. 12:1–10; Mark 6:1–6

Seasonal Color:
Green

Jesus' friends and neighbors are astonished at his teaching. They wonder about the source of his wisdom, and his authority to perform mighty works. He is only a carpenter's son. They can't accept him. Jesus replies to their put-down in words now familiar to all: "A prophet is not without honor except in his own country, and among his own kin, and in his own house." We too downgrade the gifts of those nearest us, and no marvels of grace can be performed in our midst.

Call to Worship
LEADER: I will sing of thy steadfast love, O God, for ever; with my mouth I will proclaim thy faithfulness to all generations.
RESPONSE: For thy steadfast love was established for ever, thy faithfulness is firm as the heavens.
LEADER: Let us worship God.

Prayer of Praise and Adoration
Your faithfulness is as firm as the heavens, O God; righteousness and justice are the foundation of your throne. Your steadfast love goes before you as you set the planets in orbit and establish your covenant here on earth. You still the raging waters, and calm perturbed hearts. You are God above, beyond, and within all creation. We extol you, our God, the Rock of our salvation.

Prayer of Confession
UNISON: Forgive us, O God, for our self-important boasting. We take credit for our strength without thought of your gifts. When honors are bestowed, we treat them as our due. We claim as our victories the triumphs of your grace. You shower us with blessings, which we ignore. You bring new life; we take it for granted. Deliver us from our vain ways, and forgive our smug complacency. Turn our boasting to thanksgiving for Christ's power within us.

Assurance of Pardon
LEADER: Paul declares that "when we were dead through our trespasses, God made us alive together with Christ. . . . For by

grace you have been saved through faith; and this is not your own doing, it is the gift of God . . . lest any one should boast." Let us then boast of God's grace within us, and claim with assurance the new life in Christ.

Prayer of Dedication

God of steadfast love and faithfulness, who made a covenant with the house of David, we bring our gifts so that your covenant with him may be extended throughout the world. We offer ourselves here as temples of your chosen one, David's royal son, Jesus Christ. Alive in the Spirit and empowered by service, we go forth in his name to proclaim your love as a sanctuary for those who are in need.

Prayer of Thanksgiving

O God, we give you thanks for Jesus, whose word enlightens our lives. He wrought mighty works and taught what it meant to have faith. He relied on a greater authority than that granted by earthly rulers, and freed us from bondage to principalities and powers. Though he was a stranger among his own, we proclaim him our savior and serve him as members of his true family.

We give thanks for strangers and all those whose behavior challenges the accepted norm. In them we can learn what it means to be led by the Spirit. They can show us how to discern your will as they respond to your living word. Their freedom can release us from standard morality and dead rules.

We give thanks for those whom others do not honor, angels of mercy who desire only to be useful to you. Their strength comes from the abiding sense of your indwelling Spirit. From them we learn how to love one another and to overcome selfishness.

Through strangers and angels you show us a better way. There is much we will never comprehend, but in Christ you have made known your love once and for all. For the gift of love and for loving ones, we give you thanks.

EIGHTH SUNDAY AFTER PENTECOST

Lectionary Readings for the Day
Ps. 132:11–18; II Sam. 7:18–29   *Seasonal Color:*
Eph. 1:1–10; Mark 6:7–13   *Green*

Jesus instructs his disciples as he sends them out to preach repentance. They should travel lightly, lest their baggage hinder their ability to move freely. They should stay in one place, and not be too concerned about personal comfort. They should leave quietly if refused hospitality, and not engage in violence or retaliation. They are given authority to heal, anoint, and proclaim that God's day is at hand. We have here a checklist for discipleship as we go forth to serve.

Call to Worship
LEADER: To the saints who are also faithful in Christ Jesus: Grace and peace be unto you from God and our Savior Jesus the Christ.

RESPONSE: Blessed be God, who in Christ chose us before the world was founded. In Christ we may stand holy and blameless before God.

(Author's adaptation)

LEADER: Let us worship God.

Prayer of Praise and Adoration
O God, we worship and praise you for your gift of redemption. In Christ you chose us before the world was created. You sent him to cleanse us of all our unrighteousness. He sacrificed himself for us that we should be blameless. Your grace surrounds us, and your peace dwells within us. Through Christ, who calls us and names us as your chosen people, we gather to praise you for your glorious grace.

Prayer of Confession
UNISON: God of redeeming grace, have mercy upon us as we confess our sin. Charged to travel light, we overburden ourselves. Commissioned to preach repentance, we ourselves do not change. Cautioned to avoid violence, we are quick to comfort others. Called to be reconcilers, we create divisions. As Christ sends us forth and equips us to serve him, cleanse us of abusing his trust and his name.

Assurance of Pardon

LEADER: Remember that we have redemption through Christ's sacrifice on our behalf. We have forgiveness of sins, according to riches of God's grace. For God has made known to us in all wisdom and insight the mystery of God's will, "to unite all things in him, things in heaven and things on earth." Therein lies our assurance of pardon.

Prayer of Dedication

Great God, you called a people and in Christ named us to serve you. We present ourselves in response to your mercy. Magnify your name through our thoughts and actions, so that we may reflect your goodness in all we do. Let the seal of our baptism be your stamp of approval, so that engrafted into Christ's body we can respond to his will.

Prayer of Thanksgiving

God of David and the house of Israel, who confirmed your love for all people in the gift of a Savior, who are we that we should be so blessed by your grace? Yet in him we have been set apart as a chosen race, a royal priesthood, God's own people, called and sent into the world. We who are nothing apart from your saving mercy may yet stand holy and blameless before you, because of your grace shown in Jesus Christ.

We thank you for the household of Christ, called the church. In your infinite wisdom you have brought together a multitude of peoples and cultures and made them one family through baptism. Together we proclaim one Savior, Jesus Christ, and one faith. We give thanks for this universal witness to Christ's resurrection, and pray for the day when all Christians may join as one around the Table.

Thanks be to you, O God, for one Holy Spirit, who empowers each of us with gifts according to our individual strengths and abilities. We give thanks for those with voice and those with vision, for those called to teach and those who manage. We praise you that your Spirit enables each to labor and affirms us all as workers together in Christ.

We are grateful for the world into which Christ sends us. Its beauty and grandeur inspire us, its hunger and poverty challenge us to service and sacrifice. Make us sensitive to the cries of the needy, and resourceful in ways to serve them, for the sake of him who has redeemed us by his blood.

NINTH SUNDAY AFTER PENTECOST

Lectionary Readings for the Day
Ps. 53; II Sam. 11:1–15
Eph. 2:11–22; Mark 6:30–34

Seasonal Color:
Green

Upon their return from serving and teaching, the disciples withdraw with Jesus to a lonely place. They need leisure and time for renewal, but this time it is denied them. The throngs watch where they go and get there before them. Amid the demands of the gospel, draw apart each day to commune with Christ and reflect on his teaching. Only in this way can you be renewed and equipped for ministry.

Call to Worship
LEADER: Now in Christ Jesus you who once were far off have been brought near in the blood of Christ.
RESPONSE: So then you are no longer strangers and sojourners, but citizens with the saints and members of the household of God.
LEADER: Let us worship God.

Prayer of Praise and Adoration
O God of promise, who in Christ assembled the alienated and the excluded into the folds of your compassion, we give you praise for your redeeming grace. You break down dividing walls of hostility, and fill us with your Spirit of reconciling love. You set our feet firmly on the foundation of your goodness, and impart to us wisdom that enlightens our days. You are God, who indeed promises new life to all.

Prayer of Confession
UNISON: O God, sustained by your mercy we make bold to confess our sin. We expel strangers and deny hospitality. We judge others all too freely. Our hasty words cause conflict and tension. We are disturbers of your peace. As you sent Christ to reconcile your people, forgive the failings of our unredeemed humanity and show us once again the image of your Son, who loved his enemies and taught us to do the same.

Assurance of Pardon
LEADER: Christ "is our peace, who has made us both one, and has broken down the dividing wall of hostility, by abolishing in

his flesh the law of commandments and ordinances, that he
. . . might reconcile us both to God in one body through the cross,
thereby bringing the hostility to an end." As we dwell in Christ,
so let us also receive his forgiveness of our sins.

Prayer of Dedication

Merciful Deliverer, you do not cast away your disobedient
people but receive them blameless through Christ's all-encompassing sacrifice. We come before you made clean by your righteousness. As you redeem us, you also empower us through the
gift of your Holy Spirit. We rejoice at how you restore the fortunes of your people, and bring you gifts in response to your love.

Prayer of Thanksgiving

Where would we be without your compassion, O God? Who
could stand before your judgment? Yet you promised that you
would never forsake us. You sent Christ as a sign of your faithfulness and a seal of salvation. He is a haven of hope and a source
of rest for souls weary from strife and wrongdoing. We give
thanks that he dwells by your side, there to intercede for us as
we offer our prayers.

We give thanks that he taught his disciples to draw apart for
prayer and quiet. As he walked the earth and sought time away
from the demands of the crowd, we too need to learn how to "be
still, and know that you are God." In trying to please others, we
do not replenish our resources. Encourage us to take time for
contemplation. Instill in us the discipline to reflect on your will.

We give thanks for the strength others give us as their spirits
support us and make us glad. When we are exhausted, it is they
who uplift us; when we are bent low, they help us stand tall.
Keep us from taking their concern for granted and from burden-
ing them with our problems beyond what they can bear.

Our righteousness Christ won through his sacrifice for us. Your
patience sustains as your Spirit consoles and guides us. Your
commandments nourish us as we glimpse your will for our lives.
We are surrounded by hosts of those who support us. For your
eternal revelation and these continuing reminders of your boundless compassion, we give you thanks, O God.

TENTH SUNDAY AFTER PENTECOST

Lectionary Readings for the Day
Ps. 32; II Sam. 12:1–14
Eph. 3:14–21; John 6:1–15

Seasonal Color:
Green

Feeding the multitude is a miracle. Who would have guessed that so little can satisfy so many? Five loaves and two fish show the ways of God's economy, that what is needed will be provided. Indeed, there is more than enough, and what is left is gathered. Another day will come, and there will be more people to feed. Jesus knows the reality of God's encompassing care; there will be sufficient for today and enough for tomorrow.

Call to Worship
LEADER: In God be glad, and rejoice, O righteous, and shout for joy, all you upright in heart!
RESPONSE: You are a hiding place for me, you preserve me from trouble; you encompass me with deliverance, O God most high.

(Author's adaptation)

LEADER: Let us worship God.

Prayer of Praise and Adoration
O God of deliverance, our knees bow down before you; with our voices we sing you praises. Our hands are uplifted to give you honor; our eyes are opened to behold your blessings. You are merciful in providing us a haven; you are caring and know all our needs; your presence is our assurance that you accept our worship. Send forth your Spirit, and touch all who wait before you.

Prayer of Confession
UNISON: Blessed Redeemer, have mercy upon us as we confess our sin. You endow us with goodness while we squander your blessings. We yearn for the possessions that our neighbors enjoy. Envy, greed, and selfishness consume us. Satisfaction eludes us as our cravings increase. Quiet our longing for material riches, and help us trust in Jesus, who provides for our needs.

Assurance of Pardon
LEADER: And now may Christ "dwell in your hearts through faith; that you, being rooted and grounded in love, may have power to comprehend with all the saints what is the breadth and

length and height and depth, and to know the love of Christ which surpasses knowledge, that you may be filled with all the fulness of God." With that fullness will come assurance that God forgives all our sin.

Prayer of Dedication

To you, O God, be all power and glory, blessing and honor, now and forevermore. Your mercy at work within us enables us to do and be more than we could ever ask. Your Spirit surrounds us as we dwell in the shadow of your gracious deliverance. It is Christ who guides us as we go forth to serve. May all that we do reveal your benevolence, and may what we offer reflect your goodness.

Prayer of Thanksgiving and Supplication

O God of tenderness, you cradle creation in your bosom; we give you thanks for how you care for its needs. You refresh it with the same waters that are poured on us at baptism, a reminder of your covenant, which brings new life. You cleanse it through the purging presence of your Holy Spirit, as fresh breezes replace stale air. Not a day goes by without countless reminders of how you brood over what you gave birth to; nor can we go anywhere and hope to escape the touch of your judgment. You fill us with awareness of your pervasive compassion. We give thanks for your care, which surrounds us.

We pray for the young, who begin life in utter dependence, for the unborn and newborn, who drew their first nourishment from another body. We are reminded of how needful we are. Give us hearts that reach out to children. Give us wisdom to impart direction to them. Give us patience to bear their frustrations with them. Give us humility, to listen to what they have to say without judging them. Give us imagination, so that we can enter into their hopes.

We pray for your children from whom we are alienated. If it be because of hostility or anger, give to us a spirit of reconciliation sufficient to approach them and seek forgiveness. If it be because their skin color is different or their race is not ours, give us a sense of the length of Christ's table, around which all will dine and rejoice. If it be because they taunt us or otherwise cause us discomfort, give us grace enough to show them the tenderness you give to us. Make us your agents of compassion, understanding, and reconciliation. In Christ's name we pray.

ELEVENTH SUNDAY AFTER PENTECOST

Lectionary Readings for the Day
Ps. 34:11–22; II Sam. 12:15b–24
Eph. 4:1–6; John 6:24–35

Seasonal Color:
Green

Every culture has its own bread. It may be leavened or unleav-
ened, round or rectangular, flat or airy, sour dough or sweet
dough. Jesus understands the significance of bread and uses it as
a metaphor to describe God's comprehensive care for all people.
Jesus himself is the Bread of Life, who satisfies all who hunger
for righteousness.

Call to Worship
LEADER: I beg you to lead a life worthy of the calling to which
you have been called, forbearing one another in love,
eager to maintain the unity of the Spirit in the bond
of peace.

RESPONSE: There is one body and one Spirit, just as you were
called to the one hope that belongs to your call, one
Lord, one faith, one baptism, one God who is above
all and through all and in all.

LEADER: Let us worship God.

Prayer of Praise and Adoration
O God of grace and infinite goodness, you nourish us with the
bread of life and sustain us with the peace that sets our longing
hearts at rest. You fill our cup with kindness; it overflows with
the bounty of your all-encompassing care. You chose to dwell
among us and in us through our Savior, Jesus Christ. We praise
you and adore you, O God of us all.

Prayer of Confession
UNISON: God of mercy, be above us to judge us, and be within
us to convict us of our sin. Teach us who worship false gods to
fear you, the one true God. Teach us who commit evil deeds to
obey you, and you alone. Teach us who oppress our neighbors
the ways of righteousness and truth. Teach us who do not pursue
peace the futility of war and the blessings of *shalom.*

Assurance of Pardon
LEADER: God was in Christ reconciling the world, satisfying our
hunger and thirst after righteousness. Jesus is the Bread of Life.

All who come to him and humbly confess their sin will be filled with God's mercy and sustained by God's grace. So taste and see how God cares for you. Know and believe the good news of God's love.

Prayer of Dedication

O God, in Christ you call us to lead a life worthy of our calling. We come before you and implore you to accept our gifts. We offer our diversity, that it may be made one by your reconciling Spirit. We return to you the talents conferred by your creative goodness. We present to you our acts of obedience in response to your trust. May who we are and what we do be acceptable in your sight, through Christ our redeemer.

Prayer of Thanksgiving

O God, who chose to dwell among us in Jesus Christ, we give thanks that we can behold your glory and learn of your will. As Jesus taught of old in the synagogue, so your truth is made known today in pulpit and classroom. We give thanks for this ageless wisdom set in the context of history, a history which belonged to those who went before us, which is ours today, and which will be for those who come after us. As you judged David, so also you judge us today. As David repented and worshiped you, so also have we confessed and been cleansed.

We give thanks that you have chosen us as your covenant people. You have taken these earthen vessels and transformed them, molding and fitting us to conform to your purpose. You have fired us with your Spirit, and given each unique talents. Though diverse, we are one through Christ. We give you thanks that your Spirit continues to inspire us to use your gifts. It is the Holy Spirit who takes what seems impossible and makes it become reality.

We give thanks that in you we can truly be servants. In Christ you have shown us how to serve neighbors, to carry with us the towel and the basin of hospitality, to empty ourselves of superficial vanity, which impedes our reacting to those who are hurt, and to be filled with conviction to see justice realized. Aware of the responsibility of being chosen, we go forth with thanksgiving for our one baptism, for the Spirit who guides us, and for your Kingdom, which reigns over all.

TWELFTH SUNDAY AFTER PENTECOST

Lectionary Readings for the Day
Ps. 143:1–8; II Sam. 18:1, 5, 9–15
Eph. 4:25 to 5:2; John 6:35, 41–51

Seasonal Color:
Green

Jesus is aware that whatever authority he possesses God has bestowed on him. It is God working in him that enables him to call disciples to follow. Those who respond will learn God's will, obey God's commandments, receive the Bread of Eternal Life, and be guided throughout their days by the Holy Spirit. Answer God's call, become followers of Christ, and you will receive whatever is needed for the journey of faith!

Call to Worship
LEADER: Hear my prayer, O God; give ear to my supplications! In thy faithfulness answer me, in thy righteousness!
RESPONSE: Let me hear in the morning of thy steadfast love, for in thee I put my trust. Teach me the way I should go, for to thee I lift up my soul.
LEADER: Let us worship God.

Prayer of Praise and Adoration
Your mercy is fresh every morning, O God; your ways are just and true. You cause the day to dawn with the promise of life everlasting; in Christ we learn of your will. Your Spirit surrounds us with wisdom and guidance; you do not forsake us when we seek your counsel. Be pleased as we praise you, and make haste to hear us, for we assemble to honor you, God of new life.

Litany of Confession and Assurance of Pardon
LEADER: Therefore, since we are members one of another, put away falsehood and speak the truth.
RESPONSE: Forgive us, O God, for we deceive one another.
LEADER: Be angry, but do not sin; do not let the sun go down on your anger.
RESPONSE: Forgive us, O God, since we are prone to hold grudges.
LEADER: Do not steal, but work honestly; make yourselves able to give to those in need.
RESPONSE: Forgive us, O God, for we squander your mercies and take no delight in sharing our means.

LEADER: Let no evil talk come out of your mouths, only talk that builds up your neighbor.

RESPONSE: Forgive us, O God, for we slander one another without being conscious of the destruction we cause.

LEADER: Know that Christ loved us and gave himself for us, a fragrant offering and sacrifice to God.

RESPONSE: If we are sorry and truly repent of our sin, in Jesus Christ we are forgiven.

(Author's adaptation)

Prayer of Dedication

Eternal God, who gave us Jesus Christ, the Bread of Life, we respond to your goodness by offering ourselves as dough to be made alive by the leaven of the gospel. Knead us and mold us to fit your will for us. Flavor us with the richness of Christ's teaching, shape us by his sacrificial love on our behalf, infuse us with your Spirit, and send us forth to be bread for the world.

Prayer of Thanksgiving and Supplication

O God, we give you thanks for the household of faith. Your authority establishes it; your promise gives it assurance of your abiding presence; your Messenger, Jesus Christ, calls us to live as its members; your Spirit pervades and enlivens it. We give thanks for those who have lived before us as heirs of your goodness. They have passed on their vision to us. From them we receive examples of faithfulness as they responded to Christ's teachings; through them we are aware of your comfort during times of trial and temptation; because of them we may face boldly the times that await us, led by their insight and upheld by their courage. As Christ calls us and names us, we seek to follow their example of loyalty and devotion. Look with favor upon us as we offer our prayer.

Make us more conscious of those who yearn to hear your word, who seek direction for otherwise aimless lives. Let us be for them the clear call to commitment, a source of hope and meaning in the midst of change and dislocation. Lead us together to new respect for the mysteries of faith that defy easy comprehension and marginal discipline. Guide us in our probing to be confronted with that sense of your grandeur and our own limited and temporal existence. Help us to follow in the footsteps of saints who dwell eternally at your throne of grace. May the course they charted direct our pilgrimage, and the lessons they learned remain a heritage that we can pass on to those who come after us.

THIRTEENTH SUNDAY AFTER PENTECOST

Lectionary Readings for the Day
Ps. 102:1–12; II Sam. 18:24–33

Eph. 5:15–20; John 6:51–58

Seasonal Color:
Green

"When we break the bread, is it not a sharing in the body of Christ? When we give thanks over the cup, is it not a sharing in the blood of Christ?"* These are words spoken as a minister takes the loaf, breaks it in full view of the congregation, and then pours the fruit of the vine into the cup. The bread and the cup are gifts of God for the people of God.

Call to Worship
LEADER: Hear our prayer, O God. Let our cry come to thee!

RESPONSE: Incline your ear to us, answer us speedily in the day when we call!

LEADER: Let us worship God.

Prayer of Praise and Adoration
Eternal God, your mercy is everlasting, your goodness eternal; your name endures to all generations. As we gaze at the stars, they dance to your music; the moon shines, reflecting your glory. We greet the sunrise and rejoice in creation. Tasting the rain, we affirm how you care for us; touching the sand, we are in awe of your power. You enliven our senses to the scope of your grandeur. We give you all honor as we worship your name.

Prayer of Confession
UNISON: O God, deliver us from the burden of sin as we make our confession. Remove the scales from our eyes, for we overlook neighbors in need. Cleanse us of selfishness, which keeps us from serving them. Purge us of vanity, since we expect them to be grateful. Help us not to brood over the seeming ingratitude of some we serve. Restore us by Christ's redeeming sacrifice, and purify our intentions. Make us fit for your service. In Christ's name we pray.

Assurance of Pardon
LEADER: Jesus has said, "I am the light of the world; those who follow me will not walk in darkness, but will have the light of

---

*Joint Office of Worship, Presbyterian Church (U.S.A.) and the Cumberland Presbyterian Church, *The Service for the Lord's Day,* pp. 126–127. Westminster Press, 1984.

life." "Therefore, it is said, 'Awake, O sleeper, and arise from the dead, and Christ shall give you light.'" Arise, walk in the light. In Christ you are forgiven.

Prayer of Dedication

Eternal God, you redeem us in Jesus; we can boldly approach you. Sustained by his word to us, we are enabled to serve. Impelled by your Spirit, we respond to your commands. Direct us and guide us as we seek to accomplish your will. We bring our offerings; use them for your purpose. We dedicate our time; fill it with your presence. We give ourselves; satisfy your intentions. All that we have, we present unto you.

Prayer of Thanksgiving and Petition

O God of tender mercies, we give thanks for the example of David, who grieves for Absalom, his son; for the psalmist, who laments his condition before you; for Jesus, who is touched by all who were afflicted; and for Paul, whose suffering never keeps him from proclaiming the good news. Give us tender hearts, and courage in the face of sorrow and personal pain.

We pray for those who grieve the loss of a loved one. Surround them with your embracing compassion; care for them in their solitude, and comfort them during the lonely hours. May the Spirit of the living Christ abide with them to encourage them, and may Christ's resurrection from death give them hope for life that lasts eternally.

We pray for those who lament their condition. Hear them as they plead for some sign of relief. Help us to sit with them and soothe their anxiety, to understand them in a way that will bring consolation. Keep us from denying them amid their affliction, from shaming them or compounding their burden. May we be for them the balm that anoints them with courage.

We pray for those afflicted with sundry ailments. Send Christ's healing power, which can restore them to wholeness. Use us as instruments of your mercy, so that we sit with the lonely, feed the hungry, show hospitality to the stranger, and clothe the naked. Grant those who are healers the patience to allow your miraculous powers to work, O God, and those who are sick the resources to cope with pain and discomfort. Give to all your people the hope, confidence, and dignity that come from being children of God.

FOURTEENTH SUNDAY AFTER PENTECOST

Lectionary Readings for the Day

Ps. 67; II Sam. 23:1–7

Eph. 5:21–33; John 6:55–69

Seasonal Color:
Green

Jesus speaks the words of eternal life. He offers himself as spiritual food. Christ provides us with all that is necessary; we are able to proceed on the journey of faith. The words will guide us toward the right path to take. They will keep us from becoming wayward or getting lost along the way. The food will sustain us and satisfy our hunger. Christ is our guide and provider!

Call to Worship

LEADER: God, be gracious to us and bless us and make your face to shine upon us.

RESPONSE: That your way may be known upon earth, and your saving power among all nations.

LEADER: Let the peoples give you praise, O God; let all the peoples give you praise.

(Author's adaptation)

Prayer of Praise and Adoration

All blessing, glory, and honor be unto you, O God, for your way guides our behavior, and your saving power redeems us when we stray. You are beneath us as a sure foundation. You are above us as a canopy of light. You go before us as a revealer and guide. You stand behind us as the source of righteousness and peace. God of all that was, is, and shall be, we praise and adore you.

Prayer of Confession

UNISON: O God, redeem us, for we stand in need of forgiveness. We squander your mercy when we abuse your creation. We slander our neighbors and seek not your peace. Nations rise up against nations, and threats of war fill the air. Those without work find no hope of relief. The homeless wander without protection from harm. Christ had compassion on all those who suffered. Cleanse us of the sin that closes our hearts to our brothers and sisters.

Assurance of Pardon

LEADER: Know that God hears our prayer and will have mercy on all who humbly repent of their sin. Did not God send Christ our Savior to cleanse us of unrighteousness? Does not Christ intercede on behalf of those who confess? Lay aside your burden, then, and take courage from the gospel. God forgives us through Christ.

Prayer of Dedication

God of goodness and mercy, we bring you our offerings. We laud you with thanksgiving for the blessings you bestow. You fill us with hope; we give you our commitment. You instill in us confidence; we offer our trust. You teach us how to sacrifice; we seek to be faithful. You call us to obey you; we pledge our allegiance. All that we have we place before you. Use us and mold us to conform to your will.

Prayer of Thanksgiving

Merciful God, who in Jesus Christ established the household of faith, we praise you for those in whose midst we are privileged to dwell. We give thanks for relatives who surround us with love. You created us dependent upon others for our nurture and growth. You gave us parents and guardians to care for us, siblings and age peers as companions along the way. We give thanks for our homes and the names we bear.

We are heartily thankful as well for partners and lovers, who share our sorrows and our joys, and for the young and the old, who season our lives with wisdom and verve. As Jesus chose a few in whom to confide, so we are grateful for those we can trust.

We give thanks for friends who cheer us on. In them we see your Spirit of counsel and might. They stand beside us to encourage us when we are doubtful. They go before us to mark a trail we can follow. They stand behind us to push when we are indecisive, and they hold us up when we are weighed down with trouble. For all those named and unnamed who surround us with compassion and patience, we give you thanks. Reflecting the splendor of your grace, the richness of your benevolence, and the scope of your love, we join together with those in Christ's household committed to serving you as the family of faith.

FIFTEENTH SUNDAY AFTER PENTECOST

Lectionary Readings for the Day
Ps. 121; I Kings 2:1–4, 10–12

Eph. 6:10–20; Mark 7:1–8, 14–15, 21–23

Seasonal Color:

Green

What pollutes? Is it what we take into our systems or what we ourselves generate? Jesus declares it is the latter and warns his critics to act consistently with what God commands. Ceremonial washing is meaningless if we foul the environment with evil words and deeds. It is meaningless to honor God with our lips if we do not love our neighbors as ourselves.

Call to Worship
LEADER: I lift up my eyes to the hills; from where is my help to come?

RESPONSE: My help comes from [God], the maker of heaven and earth.

(BCP)

LEADER: Let us worship God.

Prayer of Praise and Adoration
God of steadfast love, you have written your testimonies upon the hearts of your people; your commandments have guided them throughout the ages. We praise you for Jesus, who makes your will known to us. We sense your Spirit at work in our lives. Throughout all creation, you maintain your presence and give us cause for rejoicing. We acknowledge your marvelous deeds and adore you.

Prayer of Confession
UNISON: God of strength and might, we confess our neglect of salvation's armor. We have not girded our loins with truth. The breastplate of righteousness is tarnished by our lax behavior. Our feet are caked with mud from battles fought unshod by the gospel of peace. We have laid aside the shield of faith, and weakened our defense in a hostile world. Help us once again to don the helmet of salvation and to raise the sword of the word against the powers that oppose you, so that in all our struggles we may rely solely on your strength.

Assurance of Pardon
LEADER: Hear for your comfort the words of Paul: "If God is for us, who is against us? . . . For I am sure that neither death, nor

life, nor angels, nor principalities, nor things present, nor things to come, nor powers, nor height, nor depth, nor anything else in all creation, will be able to separate us from the love of God in Christ Jesus our Lord."* Accept your forgiveness and rejoice in a love stronger than our sin.

Prayer of Dedication

O God, who alone can keep us from falling, we come bearing gifts in response to your grace. Thanksgiving we offer for the mercies you give us. Glad praises we sing for the salvation Christ has won for us. Our acts we commit to your righteous judgment; we acknowledge the guidance your Holy Spirit bestows. All that we have is a gift of salvation; we commit ourselves to you in response to Christ's call.

Prayer of Thanksgiving and Supplication

Almighty God, whose testimony is sure and whose ordinances provide a stable foundation, we come with thanksgiving for the guidance your commandments impart. They are a bulwark that defends us against temptation. They are your gift to us to keep us attuned to your will for our lives. We thank you that we may walk faithfully before you, full of the wisdom you have revealed.

We give thanks for Jesus, who taught his followers the full meaning of the law. He would not allow it to constrain him from serving those in need. Help us to be bold in following his example; give us too the freedom to move beyond the law in order to fulfill it. Keep us from interpreting your commandments in ways that inhibit our ability to respond to what you intend us to do. May we see in your precepts our charge to become disciples, and hear in them your pervasive desire for our allegiance.

We give thanks for the Holy Spirit, who interprets your law in specific occasions. We are protected thereby from our own whims and desires. When we would stray from the tasks to which you call us, help us sense your Spirit frustrating our attempts. When our own insights fail us, or we are misled by the counsel of others, give us the patience to wait for your direction, and the strength to heed it.

Gird us, O God, once again with the truth of Christ's gospel. Make our feet ready to do whatever is necessary to bring peace. Armed with the breastplate of your reconciling forgiveness, we go forth as ambassadors, your Kingdom to proclaim.

*Rom. 8:31, 38–39.

SIXTEENTH SUNDAY AFTER PENTECOST

Lectionary Readings for the Day
Ps. 119:129–136; Prov. 2:1–8
James 1:17–27; Mark 7:31–37

Seasonal Color:
Green

Jesus made the "deaf hear and the dumb speak." There are many blocks to our hearing and speaking. Attentive listening is necessary before we can clearly proclaim the good news of salvation. Amid society's clamor, listen for what God intends and then, without stammering, boldly announce the hope of the gospel.

Call to Worship
LEADER: Your decrees are wonderful, [O God]; therefore I obey them with all my heart.

RESPONSE: Turn to me in mercy, as you always do to those who love your Name.

(BCP)

LEADER: Let us worship God.

Prayer of Praise and Adoration
Make your face to shine upon us, O God, and be pleased to dwell in our presence. We gather before you to give you our praise. Our ears have been opened to the sounds of angels singing hosannas; our tongues have been loosed to shout "Alleluia! Amen!" We listen attentively for your word, which brings wisdom. We wait expectantly to confess anew our allegiance in faith. Make your face to shine upon us, O God, and be pleased with our worship.

Prayer of Confession
UNISON: O God, giver of mercy, in Christ's name hear us as we confess our sin. We speak when we should listen; we hesitate when we should act. Anger prevents us from working your righteousness; selfishness inhibits our responding in faith. We are called to proclaim boldly the dawn of your Kingdom, but our shouts turn out to be mere whispers. Cleanse us of wickedness, and fill us with meekness. Redeem us in Christ, in whose name we pray.

Assurance of Pardon
LEADER: Remember that "as many of you as were baptized into Christ have put on Christ. There is neither Jew nor Greek, there

is neither slave nor free, there is neither male nor female; for you are all one in Christ Jesus."* So live as free people, abounding in the hope of the gospel, for in Jesus Christ you are forgiven.

Prayer of Dedication
Gracious God, accept the tributes we bring, and bless our endeavors in your name. With our voices we will sing your praises; with our hands we will care for the suffering. With our feet we will seek to walk faithfully; with our hearts we will love you completely. All that we have we return to you, who endow us with bountiful gifts.

Prayer of Thanksgiving
O God, you drape our shoulders with the mantle of your protection; we give you thanks for the countless ways you care for creation. Through our Savior, the Christ, you have cast away doubt and fear, even of death itself, and loosened the chains of our ultimate bondage. We give thanks for his Spirit, who dwells within us and around us and surrounds us with truth as we pursue the way of your glorious Kingdom.

We are thankful for Christ, who has opened the portals of heaven and enables us daily to catch a glimpse of your glory. Through his sacrifice once and for all, he delivered us from striving after our own righteousness. We give thanks that by his grace he invites us to partake of the fruits of your mercy. As baptism is a sign of cleansing, help us to walk daily in newness of life. As the bread is broken and offered as sustenance, keep us ever mindful of those who still hunger. As the cup of blessing is passed, deepen our commitment to serve those who thirst after righteousness.

We are thankful for our companions in this pilgrimage of faith: *thinkers,* who ponder your mysteries and point to new boundaries of truth and understanding; *doers* of the word, who press on with ceaseless energy to fulfill the Kingdom's goals; *healers,* who translate the compassion of Christ into acts of human renewal and restoration. All these prepare the way for us as we journey to your new day.

*Gal. 3:27–28.

SEVENTEENTH SUNDAY AFTER PENTECOST

Lectionary Readings for the Day
Ps. 125; Prov. 22:1–2, 8–9
James 2:1–5, 8–10, 14–18; Mark 8:27–38

Seasonal Color:
Green

Jesus asks his disciples, "Who do people say that I am?" They answer, "John the Baptist, Elijah, one of the prophets." Jesus then reveals to them the cost of discipleship. To follow him will involve self-denial, sacrifice, and obedience. Such is the way of the cross!

Call to Worship
LEADER: Those who trust in God are like Mount Zion, which cannot be moved, but abides for ever.

RESPONSE: As the mountains are round about Jerusalem, so you surround your people, O God, from this time forth and for evermore.

(Author's adaptation)

LEADER: Let us worship God.

Prayer of Praise and Adoration
O God of glory, you bless the poor in spirit with the richness of your eternal favor; you choose the meek to inherit the earth. You comfort those who mourn, the hungry and thirsty you satisfy; the pure in heart catch sight of your splendor, and those who make peace you call your own. We join with the merciful, who throughout the ages have lived by your graciousness and worshiped your name.

Prayer of Confession
UNISON: God of justice and righteousness, have mercy upon us as we confess our sin. We say we love our neighbors, but we still make distinctions; we favor the rich and discount the poor. We say we have faith, but our works do not show it; we preach Jesus Christ while we send the hungry away. While our lips praise you, our hands cast off strangers. We are not worthy to ask your forgiveness except for the name of Christ, who pardoned the thief on the cross and forgave those who put him to death.

Assurance of Pardon
LEADER: Remember the words of Scripture, where it says, "Since we have confidence to enter the sanctuary by the blood of

Jesus . . . and since we have a great high priest over the house of God, let us draw near with a true heart in full assurance of faith, with our hearts sprinkled clean from an evil conscience and our bodies washed with pure water."* In Jesus Christ we are forgiven.

Prayer of Dedication

O God, in Jesus you call us to follow; we come confessing that he is the Christ. We offer ourselves to be filled with his commandments. We dedicate our actions to match his desires. We commit our intentions to be led by his Spirit. With all that we have we seek to be faithful. Accept our endeavors and bless our ambitions. Honor our commitment, in Christ's name we pray.

Prayer of Thanksgiving and Supplication

Merciful God, in Christ Jesus you call believers to the new and living way of the gospel; we give thanks that we are numbered among those so chosen. We are thankful for Peter, who testified boldly that Jesus was the Messiah, even though he was confused about what discipleship meant. From him we learn how we too need to make our confession, although we may not be clear about what you intend us to do.

Give us confidence to step up to the brink of uncertainty and face the abyss of our own doubt. We give thanks for Jesus, who could cry out for you to save him, since we too are afraid of what the future might bring. Help us to feel his comforting Spirit surrounding us, giving us assurance that we are not alone. Help us hear anew the testimony of those who have gone before us, that you do not forsake those who put their trust in you. Turn our heads from gazing on what has been the security of the past, and help us accept the vision and promise of your glorious reign.

Give us courage, then, to take those leaps of faith which will transport us from the known to the unknown, from idolatry to obedience, from selfishness to service. We give thanks for Christ, who himself spanned the chasm from death to new life. From him we learn of your will as he makes known your commandments. Through him we can obey you, since he intercedes on our behalf. Because of him we shall henceforth serve you, for he calls us to repent and follow him. Forgetting what lies behind, we can press on to approach the portals of your Kingdom and give you thanks for Jesus, who shows us forevermore the new and living way.

*Heb. 10:19, 21, 22.

EIGHTEENTH SUNDAY AFTER PENTECOST

Lectionary Readings for the Day
Ps. 27:1–6; Job 28:20–28

Seasonal Color:

James 3:13–18; Mark 9:30–37

Green

The Kingdom of Heaven turns traditional values upside down. The least become greatest, masters become servants, the first shall be last, and children set examples. Whoever receives Jesus really welcomes, not him, but God who sent him. Whatever we do in Christ's name is done not by us but by the Spirit within us. To live in God's reign is to welcome surprises. Be open to change as you believe in the gospel.

Call to Worship
LEADER: [God] is my light and my salvation; whom then shall I fear?

RESPONSE: [God] is the strength of my life; of whom then shall I be afraid?

LEADER: One thing have I asked of [God]; one thing I seek.

RESPONSE: That I may dwell in [God's] house all the days of my life.

(BCP)

LEADER: Let us worship God.

Prayer of Praise and Adoration
We seek to dwell in your presence, O God, and behold evermore the warmth of your love. For you shelter your people during their time of adversity; you cradle them in your arms when they are afraid and lonely. You beckon us to embrace you and put an end to our fearfulness. Entering your sanctuary, we give you praise for your mercy. Be pleased with our worship as we honor your name.

Prayer of Confession
UNISON: All-wise and understanding God, hear our prayer as we confess our sin. Have mercy upon us, for we are deceitful and foolish. Ambition controls our relations with others; cheating and lying help us gain more control. We are surrounded by values that bring disorder. We are victims of selfishness that distorts your truth. Save us from boasting and serving unworthy ends; save us for Christ, in whom alone abides peace.

Assurance of Pardon

LEADER: Hear the good news: In Jesus Christ we are forgiven. "For in him all the fulness of God was pleased to dwell, and through him to reconcile to himself all things, whether on earth or in heaven, making peace by the blood of his cross."* In the peace that Christ won abides our assurance of pardon.

Prayer of Dedication

Mighty Redeemer, whose judgment is righteous and whose mercy is unbounding, we bring you our offerings in response to your grace. You sent Christ, who calls us; we give you commitment. You gave the Spirit to nurture us; we enthusiastically follow. You provide the commandments as guidance; we seek to obey you. Take us and use us to fulfill your will.

Prayer of Thanksgiving

God of all wisdom, you put the stars in the heavens and assign the planets their orbits; we give you thanks for the care you bestow on the earth. As the rains fall, the soil is nurtured; as the sun shines, the plants reach upward. You also set the seasons of life to fit your purposes; you grant us years of productivity because of your grace. Our ultimate goal is to glorify you; our richest gain is to enjoy you forever.

We are thankful for Jesus, who made known your wisdom once and for all. By his healing touch, he overcame the power of disease and injury. We give you thanks that disabilities and illness can never render us incapable of knowing your love. We can face unafraid whatever befalls us, and rejoice with assurance that we shall dwell forever made whole by your touch.

We are thankful that through his sacrifice, Christ challenged the finality of death. We can henceforth trust in your eternal care of those closest to us, and look for the day when we shall be reunited with those departed, as in that day we gather around the table of Christ's heavenly banquet.

We are thankful for the Holy Spirit, who guides us through the valleys of the shadow of doubt. When we question your judgment, it is your Spirit who reveals your will to us. When we seek wisdom and understanding, it is your Spirit who sustains and nurtures us. Gently you care for us; with peace you comfort us. For all of your mercies, which are signs of your wisdom, we give you glory and thanks, O God.

*Col. 1:19–20.

NINETEENTH SUNDAY AFTER PENTECOST

Lectionary Readings for the Day

Ps. 27:7–14; Job 42:1–6   *Seasonal Color:*
James 4:13–17; 5:7–11; Mark 9:38–50   *Green*

A cup of water, a millstone, and salt are three distinct images of discipleship. A cup of water is what one offers; it portrays refreshment, cleansing, and the promise of abiding life. A millstone is what one avoids; it stands for burden, bondage, and the threat of death. Salt is how one behaves; it depicts adding zest to life, unique abilities, and distinct service. Common images characterize an exceptional ministry.

Call to Worship

LEADER: Hear my voice, O [God], when I call; have mercy on me and answer me.
RESPONSE: You speak in my heart and say, "Seek my face." Your face, [O God], will I seek.
LEADER: O tarry and await [God's] pleasure; be strong and [God] shall comfort your heart.   *(BCP, adapted)*
          Let us worship God.

Prayer of Praise and Adoration

You do not tarry, O God of all goodness, to show us your favor. You hasten to hear us whenever we call. Bathed in the brightness of your radiant love for us, we can see clearly your care for creation. Through Christ, now open our eyes to the splendor of your redeeming judgment; by the Spirit continue to lead us to behold your dazzling grace. We worship you—God, Christ, and Holy Spirit, blessed Trinity forevermore.

Prayer of Confession

UNISON: O God of mercy, you know our lives are but illusion when we dwell not in your favor. Our acts are but vapor when we obey not your will. We boast of our good deeds, and flaunt righteous behavior, but they are conceived in arrogance and born of conceit. Forgive our deception and the damage it causes. By your mercy forgive us, and through Christ make us free.

Assurance of Pardon

LEADER: Hear again the words of assurance. Christ is "the mediator of a new covenant, so that those who are called may receive the eternal inheritance, since a death has occurred which redeems them from . . . transgressions. . . . For Christ has entered . . . into heaven itself, now to appear in the presence of God on our behalf."*

Prayer of Dedication

Born anew with the hope of your redeeming grace, O God, we come before you, bearing our gifts. Use them to spread abroad the good news that in Christ resides the promise of release from captivity, hope that peace can prevail among all your people, and assurance that you usher in the dawn of a new day.

Prayer of Thanksgiving

Mystery of mysteries, whose wisdom surpasses the farthest reaches of our imagination, whose compassion comforts us when shadows lengthen and our busy lives are hushed, whose mercy restores us when we stray, we give you thanks.

You are never far from us. If we take time to acknowledge your presence among us, we can sense that you are near. As Job answered, so also we affirm that you can do all things; nothing can surpass your care for all creation. What your commandments have taught us, the prophets declared, and the poets sung of your goodness and providence, we see all about us. We praise you for your work in our midst, and will honor your name among the nations. We are thankful for your comforting presence during times that try our faith. You have shown how you accompany your people during their wilderness wanderings. They have sung of your guidance through the valley of the shadow of death. Your own Son felt your presence when he was tempted by Satan. You can be trusted; we need only rely on your guidance.

Have patience with us when we are wayward, and lead us back into the way. When we are fearful of what tomorrow may bring, reassure us through Christ's example. You who gave us our baptism as a sign of our cleansing through Christ, invite us to be nourished at the table of new life. You who spoke through the prophets of promised deliverance, now send your Spirit to accompany us as we seek the paths of righteousness. Give us a measure of your wisdom to sustain us through our pilgrimage, and lead us at the last to your promised land.

*Heb. 9:15, 24.

TWENTIETH SUNDAY AFTER PENTECOST

Lectionary Readings for the Day
Ps. 128; Gen. 2:18–24
Heb. 1:1–4; 2:9–11; Mark 10:2–16

Seasonal Color:
Green

.A child's faith is a lesson in trust. Jesus uses such trust as an attitude befitting God's Kingdom. Children depend on others to feed them, clothe them, care for them, and instruct them. Does not God know of our needs before we express them, and has not Christ proven faithful throughout the ages? Like a child, have faith that God cares for you, and trust in Christ, who intercedes on our behalf.

Call to Worship
LEADER: Blessed is every one who fears God, who walks in God's ways!
RESPONSE: You shall eat the fruit of the labor of your hands; you shall be happy, and it shall be well with you.
LEADER: Let us worship God.

Prayer of Praise and Adoration
God of the ages, whose care for your children spans generations, we praise and adore you. We hear how you led Israel through their wanderings and brought them safely to the promised land. We are taught that Christ calls us to enter your covenant, that you open your Kingdom to all who believe him. We take part in your graciousness and live by your mercy. Hear our worship of you as we confess our faith anew.

Prayer of Confession
UNISON: O God of creation, you entrust us as stewards; we confess our abuse of what you place in our care. We foul the water by deliberate disposal; the air is polluted with emissions we create. We burn the forests through carelessness; the oceans are poisoned with toxins. Forgive our neglect of nature's delicate balance, and have mercy upon us as we renew our commitment to the created order.

Assurance of Pardon
LEADER: As we confess our sin we see Jesus, "who for a little while was made lower than the angels, crowned with glory and honor because of the suffering of death, so that by the grace of

God he might taste death for every one." Now be assured that "Christ who sanctifies and those who are sanctified have all one origin." In Jesus Christ we are forgiven.

Prayer of Dedication

God who creates us, Christ who redeems us, Holy Spirit who fills us with wondrous gifts, we come, blessed Trinity, with our tithes and our offerings. Accept them and use them to further your Kingdom. Grant that they may enlighten a corner of darkness and bring the truth of your love to those seeking freedom from bondage.

Prayer of Thanksgiving and Supplication

God of wonders, in many and various ways you speak to your people. We give thanks that you speak to us through Jesus Christ, the eternal Word made flesh. He who was with you at creation now upholds it by your providence, offering redemption for our sin, cleansing us of unworthy behavior, reconciling all things unto you, and promising peace. We give you thanks that he pioneered our salvation through suffering on behalf of all your people, and that he now sits at your right hand to intercede on our behalf when we pray.

Hear us then, as in his name we make our common supplications unto you. Teach us to trust that in your providence you will care for our needs. Quiet fears within us, when events do not occur according to our will. Help us to be less self-centered in our lives and more free to respond to your will for us. Then as we hear Christ's call to obedience, enable us to be converted by the destiny to which you call us, shaped to conform to your commandments, and sent forth to follow as his faithful disciples.

Help us to regain a child's sense of wonder and awe for your created order. Teach us to marvel at its intricate balance, rather than interfere. Lead us to work within it, since we are subject to it for our own health and well-being. Renew within us the commitment to stewardship, whereby all that we do becomes a response to the sacred trust inherited in Christ's name. To the end that your name is praised and you gain the glory, we offer our prayer and give you our lives.

TWENTY-FIRST SUNDAY AFTER PENTECOST

Lectionary Readings for the Day
Ps. 90:1–12; Gen. 3:8–19
Heb. 4:1–3, 9–13; Mark 10:17–30

Seasonal Color:
Green

Discipleship involves sacrifice as well as obedience. One without the other is never complete. Sacrifice without obedience is an empty gesture, however costly. Obedience without sacrifice is to behave in such a way that personal comfort is not disturbed. Jesus was obedient even unto death on the cross, so that those who believe in him might receive the gift of eternal life.

Call to Worship
LEADER: Before the mountains were brought forth, or the land and the earth were born, from age to age you are God.
RESPONSE: So teach us to number our days that we may apply our hearts to wisdom.

(BCP)

LEADER: Let us worship God.

Prayer of Praise and Adoration
Eternal God, you have been our resting place through the ages. Generations come and pass away, but you abide forever. We praise you for your presence among us. You bring us comfort amid our trials, clarity where confusion persists, peace in the midst of conflict, and hope of eternal life. Hear us now as we pay you our tribute, in glad adoration that you are God of our lives.

Prayer of Confession
UNISON: God who creates us, Christ who redeems us, Spirit who renews us, hear our confession. We hide from you when we should heed you; your voice we neglect. Disobedience hinders our being more faithful; we claim that others mislead us when we stray from your will, but it is our doing. Have mercy upon us and grant us forgiveness, that we may rest in your peace.

Assurance of Pardon
LEADER: Scripture reminds us that "in the days of his flesh, Jesus offered up prayers and supplications, with loud cries and tears, . . . and he was heard for his godly fear. Although he was a Son, he learned obedience through what he suffered; and being made

perfect he became the source of eternal salvation to all who obey him."* In Jesus Christ, we are forgiven.

Prayer of Dedication

God of grace and mercy, we sing you our praises, we recite our confessions, we offer our commitment in response to your love. You did not spare your only Son, but gave him up so that we may be saved. We pledge our trust in Christ to deliver us worthy of your call to discipleship. Accept what we give you as signs of obedience, and bless our efforts as we seek to be faithful.

Prayer of Thanksgiving and Supplication

God of all ages and of every generation, whose wisdom extends beyond the horizon and whose care reaches the farthest depths of the sea, we give thanks that we abide in the shelter of your encompassing love. We hear how nothing, not even death itself, can separate us from resting eternally in your presence. We give thanks for Christ's sacrifice on our behalf, how he arose victorious from the fetters of that ultimate bondage and now prepares a place for us by your side.

We pray, O God, that you will remove from us any encumbrances that keep us from realizing our destiny. Remove the scales from our eyes so that we can see clearly what you would have us do. Help us to put our trust in Christ, who alone can keep us from falling by the wayside of self-deception, avarice, false pride, or boredom. Let our faltering steps be strengthened by his willingness to suffer defeat on our behalf, so that we can henceforth walk boldly in his name.

Cleanse us of whatever foolishness causes us daily to betray him. When we expect him to work wonders on our behalf, remind us through the testimony of Scripture how he cared for all people. When we would serve him only at our convenience, startle us with his call to sacrifice all that we have and follow him. When we would betray him before others by our unwillingness publicly to proclaim him our Savior, send your Spirit among us to renew our commitment. O God, you have been "our dwelling place in all generations. . . . So teach us to number our days that we may get a heart of wisdom."

*Heb. 5:7–9.

127

TWENTY-SECOND SUNDAY AFTER PENTECOST

Lectionary Readings for the Day
Ps. 35:17–28; Isa. 53:7–12
Heb. 4:14–16; Mark 10:35–45

Seasonal Color:
Green

To serve other people is a high calling. It requires sensitivity, sympathy, and self-sacrifice. Sensitivity is the ability to feel and to hear another's needs. Sympathy describes willingness to share the burden. Self-sacrifice is the extent to which one will go to alleviate the need. All three are important and require discipline. That is why Jesus makes such a point of calling the disciples to serve others.

Call to Worship
LEADER: Let those who favor my cause sing out with joy and be glad; let them say always, "[God] is great."
RESPONSE: And my tongue shall be talking of your righteousness and of your praise all the day long.

(BCP)

LEADER: Let us worship God.

Prayer of Praise and Adoration
Your praise is ever on our lips, O God. Songs of joy swell within us. We gaze at creation and behold goodness; we hear of your covenant and discover righteousness. Your love is boundless, your care without limits. We enter your sanctuary to give you honor; we bow down before you with glad adoration. Receive our worship and accept our thanksgiving. You are God whom we serve evermore.

Prayer of Confession
UNISON: O God, who sent Christ to make intercession, have mercy on us as we confess our sin. He was oppressed; we afflict others. He was judged; we declare others unworthy. He was stricken; we cause others pain. He was put to death; we likewise destroy the innocent. Numbered with sinners, he bore our transgressions. Through Christ make us righteous, so that in him we can obey you.

Assurance of Pardon
LEADER: Since then we have a great high priest, Jesus Christ, who has passed through the heavens, let us hold fast our confes-

sion. For we have not a high priest who is unable to sympathize with our weaknesses, but one who in every respect has been tempted as we are, yet without sin. Let us then with confidence draw near to the throne of grace, with assurance that in Christ we are forgiven.

Prayer of Dedication

We draw near your throne of grace, O God, renewed by your mercy and enlivened by your power. You have given us the gift of a Savior so that in you "we live and move and have our being." Your Spirit resides within us as a source of encouragement and strength. Accept what we bring now as signs of our faithfulness, and bless what we do hereafter as we express our commitment.

Prayer of Thanksgiving and Intercession

O God of righteousness, who spared not your own Son but sent him to save us, we give you thanks for Jesus, who is Christ evermore. He loved us enough to suffer on our behalf; he was afflicted, yet remained faithful. We are thankful that he can sense our weaknesses, uphold us during trials, plead for us when you judge us unworthy, and reconcile us to you as he sits by your side.

We pray for those who cause us suffering, whatever the reasons. Stay in us the temptation to strike back at them. Keep us from grudges that block reconciliation. Help us to make of wrongdoing an occasion for understanding and compassion for the offender.

We pray for our enemies. Give us strength to withstand their blows. When gossip turns to slander, and envy to malice, keep us from becoming self-pitying or self-righteous. By your reconciling Spirit, replace pride with sympathy, anger with empathy, and resentment with conviction to work for justice and truth.

We pray for those who feel of no account in the world. Help them recover their dignity and use us in the process. As those who share Christ's ministry to the oppressed, equip us with the insight and skills to fulfill that task. Where systems oppress people, empower us to change them. Where persons abuse persons, give us the wisdom to redirect the lives affected. Make us useful servants of your righteousness and mirrors of your goodness, for the sake of him who gave his all for us.

TWENTY-THIRD SUNDAY AFTER PENTECOST

Lectionary Readings for the Day
Ps. 126; Jer. 31:7–9

Heb. 5:1–6; Mark 10:46–52

Seasonal Color:
Green

A blind man cries out to Jesus for mercy. Jesus asks what he wants him to do. "To see," the man says. "Your faith has made you well," replies the Master, and sends him on his way. Sight restored, he follows Jesus. What seems like a miracle to the reader is recounted as an everyday occurrence. To have faith in Jesus is to accept the fact that being restored to wholeness will become commonplace.

Call to Worship
LEADER: You fill our mouths with laughter, O God; you cause shouts of joy to come from our lips.

RESPONSE: You have done great things for us, O God; we come into your presence, singing your praises.

(Author's adaptation)

LEADER: Let us worship God.

Prayer of Praise and Adoration
Merciful God, whose benevolence extends to all corners of the planet, we give you praise. You seek the lame, that they may walk in your glory. You call the blind to behold your grandeur. You fill the hungry with good things, and offer release to those imprisoned. Your kindness follows us wherever we go. Your grateful people gather before you with glad adoration.

Prayer of Confession
UNISON: O God, who appointed Christ our high priest, may he intercede for us as we confess our sin. We are lame when we do not walk by faith. We are blind when we do not seek your truth. We crave self-fulfillment, rather than your righteousness. We are in bondage to ourselves. Through Christ, release us from our captivity, and in him forgive us.

Assurance of Pardon
LEADER: Remember that Christ did not exalt himself to be made a high priest but was appointed by God, who said to him, "You are a priest for ever." As we confess our sins, we have assurance that Christ intercedes on our behalf. God hears our prayer. Through Jesus Christ, we are forgiven.

Prayer of Dedication

God of goodness, you lavish your gifts on us. You have given us health; we dedicate our vigor to following Christ. You have given us strength; we offer our energy to serve neighbors in need. You have given us the commandments; we commit a portion of our wealth as signs of our faithfulness. Accept the tributes we bring. Use them to accomplish your will.

Prayer of Thanksgiving

Great are your works, O God; you make our hearts glad. Wherever we look we see your goodness. Throughout history you have restored the fortunes of your chosen people. In barren lands you led them to living waters. When they were hungry, you sent manna to sustain them. Those who went forth weeping returned home with shouts of joy, recounting the benefits of your wondrous love.

We give thanks for Christ, in whose name we inherit your mercy, and confess anew our faith in him as our high priest. He bore our weaknesses in his body, and thereby made us strong. We give thanks that he lives among us today to encourage the fainthearted, empower the weak, comfort the lonely, and bring release to the captives. Through him we are able to serve above and beyond our collective capacities, and for that legacy we give you thanks.

We give thanks for your Holy Spirit, who renews our flagging spirits and sends us forth with praise on our lips. In the midst of doubt, your Spirit brings clarity; when we are weary, your Spirit revives us. We can rely on your Spirit during lonely adventures; throughout our wanderings, we are never without your presence.

Our hearts beat with joy, thanks to your graciousness. Our eyes see more clearly, thanks to the vision of Christ our Savior. Our whole selves move more freely, thanks to your indwelling Spirit. We shout glad alleluias, so great are your works!

TWENTY-FOURTH SUNDAY AFTER PENTECOST

Lectionary Readings for the Day
Ps. 119:33–48; Deut. 6:1–9
Heb. 7:23–28; Mark 12:28b–34

Seasonal Color:
Green

The truth of the gospel is that what God requires, God also provides. God requires ultimate love and obedience. God provides Christ, who on our behalf has been made perfect forever. God requires that we love our neighbor as ourselves. God provides Christ, who as high priest always lives to make intercession on our behalf. In God we truly live, move, and have our being, thanks to Christ's perfect sacrifice for us.

Call to Worship
LEADER: Teach me, O God, the way of thy statutes; and I will keep it to the end.
RESPONSE: Let thy steadfast love come to me, O God, thy salvation according to thy promise.
LEADER: Let us worship God.

Prayer of Praise and Adoration
Your way is just and true, O God, and your commandments trustworthy. Your steadfast love is never far from us in the person of Jesus Christ, our Savior. In him we know your righteous judgment, your reconciling redemption, and your encompassing care for the whole of creation. Through him we shall walk humbly, live justly, and worship you joyously, God of our lives!

Responsive Prayer of Confession
LEADER: O God, give me understanding, that I may keep thy law and observe it with my whole heart.
RESPONSE: God, have mercy upon us, for we do not obey you.
LEADER: Lead me in the path of thy commandments, for I delight in it.
RESPONSE: Christ, have mercy upon us, since we take no delight in serving our neighbor.
LEADER: Turn my eyes from looking at vanities; and give me life in thy ways.
RESPONSE: God, have mercy upon us, because we are selfish and prone to evil.
LEADER: Behold, I long for thy precepts; in thy righteousness give me life!

RESPONSE: Christ, have mercy upon us, forgive us our sin, and by your grace may we walk in new life.

Assurance of Pardon

LEADER: The testimony of Scripture affirms our pardon when we hear, "How much more shall the blood of Christ, who through the eternal Spirit offered himself without blemish to God, purify your conscience from dead works to serve the living God."* In Jesus Christ, we are forgiven.

Prayer of Dedication

Redeeming God, cleansed by your mercy, sustained by your grace, and led by your righteousness, we come before you bearing our gifts. Purify them to serve your purpose, and nurture us to act according to your will, so that all we have and do may bring justice on earth.

Prayer of Thanksgiving

Merciful Creator, hear our prayer, as we give you the honor and praise due your glorious name. We thank you for Jesus, who himself offered up prayers and supplications to you. He partook of humanity so that through death he might destroy the power of evil, once and for all. He suffered on our behalf, yet without sinning. In his anguish he cried unto you that the burden of the cross be taken from his shoulders, yet he remained faithful. We give thanks that in his being made perfect, he intercedes for us.

We praise your name for his passage through heaven, that he has prepared a way for us into your glorious sanctuary. We give thanks that by his death and resurrection he tore asunder the veil that kept us from beholding your glory. He taught the commandments, and himself assured their fulfillment.

We give you thanks that in him we can faithfully walk the path of discipleship. He teaches us what it means to obey you. Because of his faithfulness, we can hold fast our confession of hope without wavering. Through his commandments we hear how to stir up one another to love and good works. By his example, we gather as his disciples to sing you psalms of adoration and feast on the sacrament which he ordained. The bread of the covenant will sustain us and nourish us through the trials that await us. The cup of new life assures us that you will never forsake us. For all that, O God, we give you the honor and praise.

*Heb. 9:14.

Lectionary Readings for the Day
Ps. 146; I Kings 17:8–16
Heb. 9:24–28; Mark 12:38–44

Seasonal Color:
Green

The widow's mite has become a symbol of stewardship. She gave not out of abundance but out of poverty. Jesus says that she gave everything she had. Stewardship is a sacred trust bestowed by God, an opportunity to care responsibly for all of God's creation. Stewardship grows out of faith that God will sufficiently care for all our needs. The widow knew what it meant to enter God's sacred trust.

Call to Worship
LEADER: Hope in God, who made heaven and earth, the sea, and all that is in them. Hope in God, who keeps faith for ever.

RESPONSE: I will praise God as long as I live; I will sing praises to my God while I have being.

(Author's adaptation)

LEADER: Let us worship God.

Prayer of Praise and Adoration
We praise you, God of all being! You give food to the hungry, set prisoners free, open the eyes of the blind, and lift the spirits of those bowed down. Because you are righteous, you sent Christ to redeem the lost and the wayward. We come into your presence enlivened by your Holy Spirit and full of new hope to give you the honor due your glorious name.

Prayer of Confession
UNISON: Merciful God of compassion and justice, take pity on us as we confess our sin. We are not the stewards Christ calls us to be. Riches possess us while others go hungry. We mismanage creation with our pollution and strife. Your goodness is betrayed by our lust for power. We abuse your provision for us by our selfish desires. Help us hear once again Christ's call to be faithful, and through him forgive us as we repent of our sin and turn from it.

Assurance of Pardon
LEADER: Remember the words of Scripture where it says, "For Christ has entered . . . into heaven itself, now to appear in the

presence of God on our behalf . . . to put away sin by the sacrifice of himself." All who repent and eagerly await him have the assurance that their sins are forgiven.

Prayer of Dedication

God of grace and glory, all that we have is a gift of your mercy. You shower blessings upon us out of your goodness. You redeem us from the evil one, and rescue us from the pit of our own selfishness. We come before you, seeking to be faithful to Christ's call to stewardship. Accept what we offer as signs of our yearning to be better caretakers of your creation.

Prayer of Thanksgiving and Supplication

Author of all creation, Sovereign over all creatures, we praise you for your goodness and give thanks for your mercy. We give thanks that in Christ Jesus you have called us to be disciples, and that you delight to fill us with your Holy Spirit, who prods us to greater faithfulness.

We give thanks for Jesus, who calls us to be caretakers of the treasures nature provides. Help us through him to relinquish our lust to control all we see. Make us responsive to what is around us, so that we sanctify the world rather than subdue it, rely on the created order and not always have to remake it, and support the natural course of events rather than always subjecting them to our own purposes.

Sanctified by Christ's sacrifice on our behalf, we give thanks for your Spirit, who reconciles us anew with your will. Through the Spirit, transform our surroundings from the mundane to the sacred, so that in all we do we can respond to your divine trust. Help us use our time wisely and to your advantage. Give us discipline to nurture the talents you give, and zeal to use them to your honor and glory.

Subject to Christ who calls us, attuned to your Spirit who empowers us, and commissioned to proclaim you Author and Finisher of all creation, we go forth to the respective scenes of our labors. Bless our intentions and sanctify our efforts. May their effects be acceptable, in Christ's name we pray.

TWENTY-SIXTH SUNDAY AFTER PENTECOST

Lectionary Readings for the Day
Ps. 145:8–13; Dan. 7:9–14
Heb. 10:11–18; Mark 13:24–32

Seasonal Color:
Green

The Word of God is eternal, surpassing all earthly knowledge. God sent the Word into the world, so that those who dwell on earth may have life, and that abundantly. Earthly life shall pass away, yet those who believe in Christ shall live eternally, for such is God's promise. Amid the trials and the burdens of mundane existence, hope in the Word, who brings order out of chaos and life beyond death.

Call to Worship
LEADER: God is gracious and merciful, slow to anger, and abounding in steadfast love.
RESPONSE: All your works shall give you thanks, O God, and all your saints shall bless you!

(Author's adaptation)

LEADER: Let us worship God.

Prayer of Praise and Adoration
God of dominion, power, glory, and honor, God of tenderness, compassion, patience, and comfort, we come extolling your virtues and praising your name. You are too wonderful for comprehension; we live because of your embracing mercy. We bless you for Christ, through whom we may know you, bow down before you, worship and adore you, God of all ages. Alleluia! Amen.

Litany of Assurance
LEADER: When Christ had offered for all time a single sacrifice for sins, he sat down at the right hand of God.
RESPONSE: In Jesus Christ, we are forgiven.
LEADER: For by a single offering he has perfected for all time those who are sanctified.
RESPONSE: In Jesus Christ, we are forgiven.
LEADER: And the Holy Spirit adds, "I will remember their sins and their misdeeds no more."
RESPONSE: In Jesus Christ, we are forgiven.
LEADER: Where there is forgiveness of these, there is no longer any offering for sin.
RESPONSE: In Jesus Christ, we are forgiven.

Prayer of Dedication

"Ancient of Days, who sittest throned in glory; To Thee all knees are bent, all voices pray; Thy love has blest the wide world's wondrous story With light and life since Eden's dawning day."* We come before you, O God, beholding your glory, and offer you gifts in praise of your name. May your light so shine that all creation discerns your dominion, and may whatever we do bring you honor and praise.

Prayer of Thanksgiving

O Triune God, whose dominion is eternal, we praise you for unwarranted blessings bestowed on your people throughout the ages. You led them through the barren places, providing food by day and protection by night. You made them wise through the voice of the prophets, and called them to account for their deeds. You gave them the Ark which contained the commandments, as a seal of your promise that they were your chosen people. We give thanks that we inherit this legacy of promise and fulfillment, and partake with our ancestors in faith of your wondrous love.

We praise you for Jesus, who calls us as heirs of your favor. It is through him that we dare to come into your presence. Once and for all he rent the veil in the heavenly sanctuary, and invites all who believe in him to come, enter in. We give thanks for the peace we receive when we follow, for the assurance that comes with your redeeming pardon. He remains with us as we seek to obey you. We give thanks for the teachings he bequeathed to his disciples, words of wisdom that continually guide us as we hear your living word proclaimed anew.

We praise you for the Spirit, who renews confidence and grants endurance for the paths of discipleship that lie ahead. We will not shy away from threatening encounters with your Spirit to guide how we ought to act. Our knees will not tremble, nor will our hands remain idle, as long as the Spirit enables response. You have seen to it, O God, that we are empowered for service. May all our works praise you, and all your saints bless you.

*The Hymnal, Hymn 58; Presbyterian Board of Christian Education, 1933.

TWENTY-SEVENTH SUNDAY AFTER PENTECOST
CHRIST THE KING

Lectionary Readings for the Day
Ps. 93; Jer. 23:1–6
Rev. 1:4b–8; John 18:33–37

Seasonal Color:
White

Again Jesus is questioned about his authority. Whence came the right to do what he did? What special insight enabled him to utter profound teachings? What source did he tap to perform healing deeds? Today it may be easier to answer such questions, but it is still as difficult to believe in his authority. Otherwise, why do some doubt him, deny him, and distrust him? Is he, or is he not, the Savior?

Call to Worship
LEADER: [God] has made the whole world so sure that it cannot be moved.
RESPONSE: Your testimonies are very sure, and holiness adorns your house, O [God], for ever and forevermore.

(BCP)

LEADER: Let us worship God.

Prayer of Praise and Adoration
O God of enduring compassion and mercy, your dominion is unending, your judgment forthright. We live by your grace, assured of your love. We praise you for Jesus, who taught how to honor you; we are awed by your Spirit, who guides and sustains us. We come into your presence to learn your will for us, to worship and adore you as we abide in your realm.

Prayer of Confession
UNISON: O God of mercy, woe be upon us, for we do not obey you. We confess one baptism, yet we foster divisions in Christ's body. We observe the Lord's Supper but work not for Christ's peace. We confess our reluctance to extend your favor to those we don't like. Forgive and restore us for the sake of your Son, Jesus Christ. You are a God of dominion; we live by your grace alone.

Assurance of Pardon
LEADER: We are told in Scripture that the days are coming when God will raise up a righteous Branch, who shall reign and deal

wisely, who shall execute justice and righteousness in the land. We believe that Christ has come and performed all that was foretold by the prophets. I can assure you that in Jesus Christ we are forgiven.

Prayer of Dedication
Source of deliverance and help, you invite us to live evermore in your favor. We offer ourselves to you in response to Christ's call. Out of the abundance of your love we offer gifts to you. From the storehouse of your mercy we bring you treasures. Accept the gleanings of our labor as we lay them before you. To you belong the glory and the dominion forever and ever.

Prayer of Thanksgiving and Intercession
Benevolent Ruler of nations and Protector of peoples, we come with thanksgiving for your mighty care. You do not draw apart from your people, but through Christ choose to dwell in our midst. We give thanks that he became the servant of humanity and stooped to the needs of the lowly and humble. In him we have assurance that you hear us when we pray, grieve with us when we are afflicted, mourn as we do the loss of loved ones, and care enough to judge and redeem us when we stray from your way.

We pray for those who govern us in society. Give to them a sense of your compassion and care. Keep them from setting themselves apart from the needs of those whom they serve, and endow them with patience and wisdom to work for the well-being of all. As we elect them to office, lead us to entrust them with sufficient authority to perform their duties. Keep us from ignoring their judgments, and help us to serve with them toward the common good of all people.

We pray for leaders of foreign lands, those aligned with us and those antagonistic toward us. Help us to work with our allies for common strength, shared benefits, and greater commitment to justice and peace. With those who are antagonistic, grant us understanding, compassion, and the humility to see their point of view. Keep us through Christ from rebuilding the walls of enmity and hostility he came to abolish. And may we through your Spirit be granted significant wisdom and courage to work peaceably with all peoples. We yearn for the time when your vision is realized, and the lion shall lie with the calf, and war shall be no more!

Index of Scripture Readings